PASTISSIMA!
Pasta the Italian Way

PASTISSIMA!
Pasta the Italian Way

Text by Leonardo Castellucci
Photography by Marco Lanza
Set Design by Cinzia Calamai

PB

PARKGATE
BOOKS

The Publishers would like to thank Mastro Ciliegia (Fiesole), Pasquinucci (Florence), La Boutique della pasta fresca (Florence), Casa pulita (Florence), for their assistance during the production of this book

First published by © McRae Books 1996
This edition published in 1997 by

Parkgate Books Ltd
London House
Great Eastern Wharf
Parkgate Road
London SW11 4NQ
Great Britain

1 3 5 7 9 8 6 4 2

Conceived, edited and designed by McRae Books, Florence, Italy

Text: Leonardo Castellucci
Photography: Marco Lanza
Set Design: Cinzia Calamai

Design: Marco Nardi
Translation from the Italian and adaptation:
Anne McRae
Editing: Alison Leach
Illustrations: Alessandro Baldanzi

ISBN 1-85585-315-9

Colour separations: RAF, Florence, Italy
Printed and bound in Italy by Grafiche Editoriali Padane, Cremona

CONTENTS

INTRODUCTION

In Italy there are entire encyclopedias devoted to pasta cookery, and our biggest challenge here was how to squeeze such a wealth of knowledge into one quite modest volume while still conveying something of the breadth of the subject. The solution seemed to be to create a book that can be used in two different ways; first as a simple set of pasta recipes, and these you will find in the main part of the book (pp.36-119), and, second, "interactively", by providing a series of basic sauces, tips on types of pasta to serve them with, and instructions on making pasta at home. By combining pasta and sauces in different ways you will be able create a wide variety of dishes. Italians are famous (or notorious) throughout the world for being creative and "flexible". This same flexibility can, and should, be brought to Italian cooking. Don't cancel the dinner party if you can't find pancetta (use bacon), gorgonzola (blue vein with a dash of fresh cream?), or fresh rosemary (try dried). The results will be different, but the important thing is to enjoy the food, both eating it and preparing it. Buon appetito!

A Short History of Pasta

Like many things, the origins of pasta are lost in the mists of prehistory. We can only assume that it was "invented" some time after our ancestors had learned to cultivate cereals and to grind them into flour. The earliest references to pasta on the Italian peninsula date from Etruscan times, before the Romans and contemporary with the Ancient Greeks. An Etruscan tomb at Cerveteri, in Tuscany, has murals with images of knives, a rolling pin, and an object that looks very similar to our modern wheel cutter, the one used for giving fluted edges to fresh pasta, such as pappardelle or tagliatelle.

Etruscan bas-relief dating from the 4th century B.C. Cerveteri, Central Itay.

In Ancient Rome it seems that only the wealthiest citizens could afford to eat pasta. In his cookbook, Apician, chef to the rich and famous of Rome, gives recipes for several dishes made with *lagane*, which was what the Romans called fresh pasta.

After the fall of Rome all traces of pasta vanished for several centuries.

At the beginning of the 12th century an Arab writer, Abu Abdallah Muhammad Idris, in a book destined for the Norman king of Sicily, Roger II, gives a very precise description of how to dry, and thus preserve, fresh pasta. Once the Sicilians had learned how to conserve this delicious food, they wasted no time in letting the mainlanders in on the secret. In Naples, Amalfi, Genoa, and many other port towns, the manufacture and sale of pasta soon became a roaring trade.

Even so, these early "Italians" (remember that the country wasn't united, and thus really "Italy" until 1870) had rather different ideas about how pasta should be served than the ones you will find in this book. Pasta was usually cooked in milk or broth and served with sugar, cheese, butter and sweet spices. It wasn't until the 18th century that some sort of order was established in culinary habits, and sweet and savoury dishes were distinguished. From that time on pasta began to be served more or less as it is today, with sauces based on tomatoes, meat and vegetables.

In the second half of this century, as Italy has become richer and more industrialised, new and sophisticated commercial pasta-making machines have been invented, and pasta is now manufactured on large scale throughout the peninsula and exported all over the world. Which brings a tip to mind; when buying pasta, always try to find an Italian-made brand. This is not exaggerated nationalism, nor are we in the pay of any local manufacturers, it's just that the combination of Italian flour, Italian water, and Italian know-how makes superior quality pasta!

DRIED PASTA

The number and variety of pasta shapes available is bewildering. Over the years any special occasion or celebration has been a good excuse to invent a new one! Add to this the fact that the same pasta shape may change its name from region to region, and the different pasta manufacturers may call the same pasta shape by different names, and you will begin to understand why you need to approach the subject with some general guidelines in mind.

The long and short pasta shapes on this page are shop-bought and made from dried hard-wheat flour and water, while the smaller soup pasta shapes may also be made from egg and soft-wheat flour.

LONG AND SHORT PASTA

All dried pasta can be divided into long or short shapes. The longer ones should be served with oil-based sauces that cling to their shapes, while many of the short pasta shapes are good with chunkier sauces that can be scooped up with the fork.

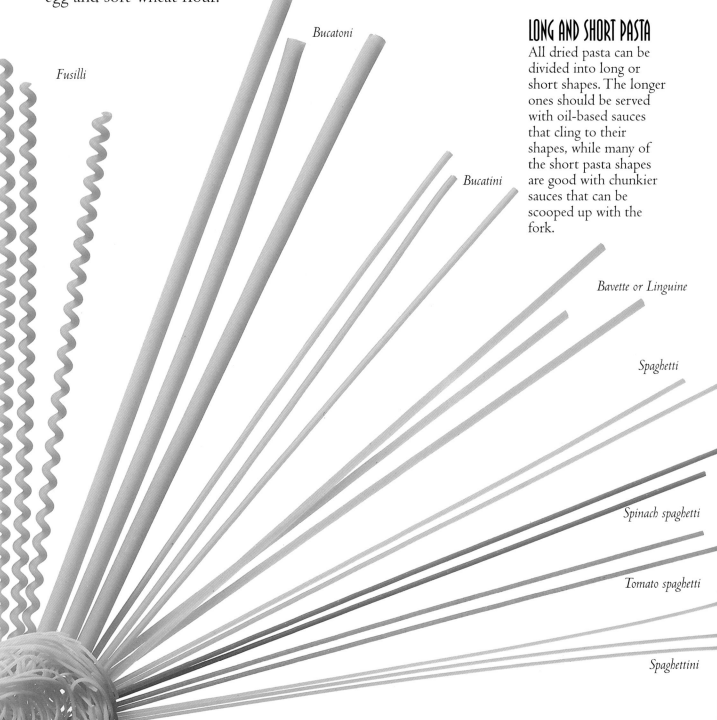

Fusilli

Bucatoni

Bucatini

Bavette or Linguine

Spaghetti

Spinach spaghetti

Tomato spaghetti

Spaghettini

Capelli d'angelo

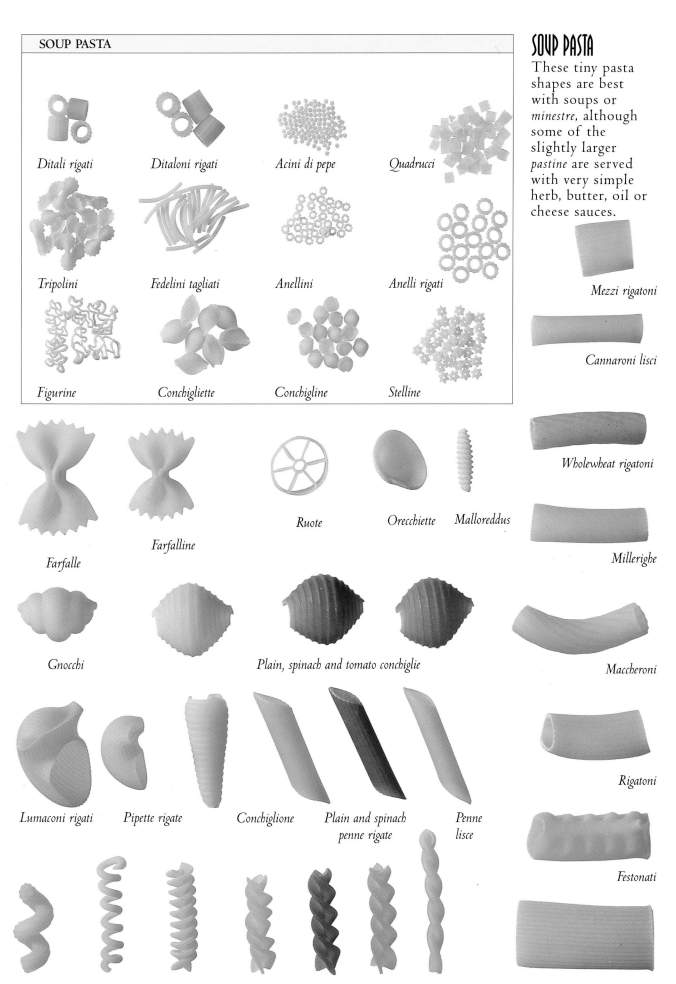

SOUP PASTA

Ditali rigati

Ditaloni rigati

Acini di pepe

Quadrucci

Tripolini

Fedelini tagliati

Anellini

Anelli rigati

Figurine

Conchigliette

Conchigline

Stelline

These tiny pasta shapes are best with soups or *minestre*, although some of the slightly larger *pastine* are served with very simple herb, butter, oil or cheese sauces.

Mezzi rigatoni

Cannaroni lisci

Wholewheat rigatoni

Millerighe

Maccheroni

Rigatoni

Festonati

Rigatoni napoletani

Farfalle

Farfalline

Ruote

Orecchiette

Malloreddus

Gnocchi

Plain, spinach and tomato conchiglie

Lumaconi rigati

Pipette rigate

Conchiglione

Plain and spinach penne rigate

Penne lisce

Cavatappi

Fusilli bucati

Fusilli

Plain, spinach and tomato eliche

Gemelli

Fresh and Filled Pasta

B y fresh pasta I mean pasta made from egg and soft-wheat flour, although the term "fresh" is somewhat misleading, since egg pasta can also be dried. In fact you will find that commercially made, dried tagliatelle, fettuccine, pappardelle, and others, are often a better (and certainly more economical) alternative to the refrigerated "fresh" pasta available in supermarkets and speciality stores. However, the best fresh pasta you can get is the homemade variety. If you have the time, and a little patience, the results will be better than anything you can buy. The added bonus is that making pasta is a very satisfying experience. See instructions on pp. 120–123. As with dried, shop-bought pasta, the names and shapes of fresh and filled pasta types vary from region to region in Italy. These are a selection of the most common types, in their most usual shapes, and sporting their more recurrent names.

FILLED PASTA

Fresh pasta can be filled with a variety of different mixtures, including meat, cheese, cheese and spinach, potatoes and other vegetables. Depending on the shape of the pasta, the results are called tortellini, tortelli, ravioli or agnolotti, to name a few.

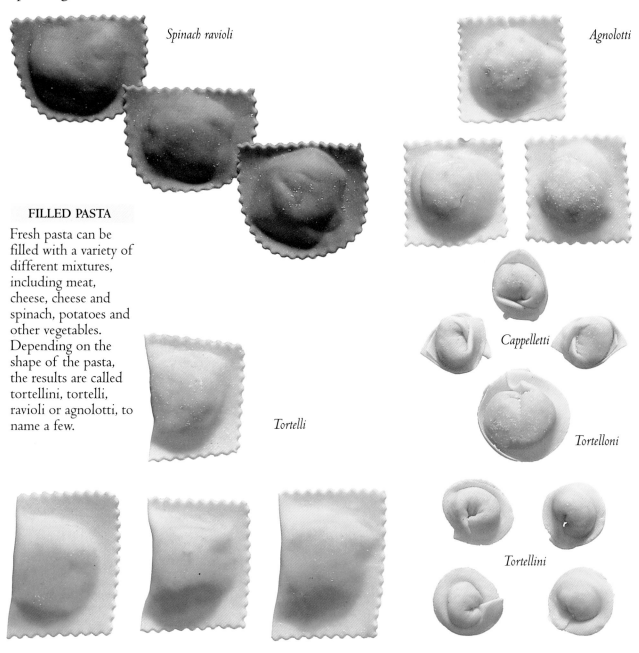

Spinach ravioli

Agnolotti

Cappelletti

Tortelli

Tortelloni

Tortellini

Pappardelle

Tagliolini

Fettuccine

Paglia e fieno

Tagliatelle

Maltagliati

Lasagne

Serving Suggestions
High quality fresh
and filled pasta are
good with simple
butter, cream or
butter and herb
sauces, well sprinkled
with freshly grated
parmesan cheese.
These simple sauces
should highlight the
delicate taste of the
egg pasta without
camouflaging it.
Mushroom, truffle,
asparagus and walnut
sauces are also good.
Other traditional
recipes include sauces
based on wild game,
such as duck, wild
boar or rabbit, as well
as tasty, well-cooked
lamb and veal.

GNOCCHI

Strictly speaking gnocchi are not pasta. In Italy preliminaries to a main course will consist of one or more *antipasti* (appetisers), followed by a *primo piatto* (first course). Pasta dishes are a typical first course but there are also many others, such as risotto, polenta, zuppe and gnocchi. Gnocchi have been included here because they are so good, and also because they are quite easy to make at home, even for beginners.

Gnocchi alla romana

Potato gnocchi

Spinach and potato gnocchi

The most common type of gnocchi, often called *topini* ("little mice"), is made of a mixture of cooked potatoes and flour, with the addition of an egg in some regions. Green gnocchi can be made of spinach and potato or spinach and ricotta. The spinach and ricotta gnocchi are called *malfatti* ("badly made") because they are made with the ingredients for stuffing ravioli but lack the pasta casing. *Gnocchi alla romana* are made with semolina and baked in the oven.

Spinach and ricotta gnocchi

SPECIAL PASTA

In recent years there has been an explosion in the number of coloured and flavoured pasta available. The purists are shocked, and I suspect that it is the tourists who are buying up most of these innovative varieties, particularly since they are sold in and around the chic, central streets of Rome and Florence, and are also widely available in souvenir shops in Tuscan hill towns. In any case, coloured pasta is fun and pretty to look at!

These are just some of the new colours and flavours available:
1   Plain
2   Basil
3   Beetroot
4   Carrot
5   Mountain herb
6   Porcini mushroom
7   Saffron
8   Squid's ink
9   Spinach
10 Salmon
11 Wholewheat
12 Tomato

Oil, Cheese and Other Ingredients

Many ingredients of classic pasta cookery, like butter, tomatoes and onions, are common throughout the world and need little introduction. Others, some of which are shown below, are more specific to the Italian pantry and may require some explanation.

OLIVE OIL

Olive oil is a fundamental ingredient in almost all pasta dishes and should be chosen with care. Buy only the highest quality oil, which is always labelled *"extra-vergine."*

Don't economize on olive oil or use other vegetable oils in its place, even for cooking. If you are on a low-fat diet, you may want to reduce the quantity of oil in the recipes a little.

WINE

Some purists still insist that wine should never be served with pasta. As you will have noticed if you have ever been to Italy, this line of thought is seriously endangered. Throughout this book I have suggested a type of wine (dry, red, white, sparkling) for most recipes. I have also suggested an Italian wine which I think will go well with the dish. These are guidelines only, and you should follow your own preferences entirely.

Meats

MORTADELLA
Mortadella is a kind of sausage made of lean pork cooked slowly to develop its special subtle blend of flavours. The best mortadella comes from Bologna and it is used in many Bolognese specialities (see tortellini, Bolognese meat sauce).

PANCETTA
Pancetta is made of pork and is comparable to an unsmoked form of bacon.

PROSCIUTTO
Prosciutto is a form of ham which has been salted and air-cured. The best kind is cured naturally over quite long periods of time (up to a year). It is never smoked.

Cheeses

Among the hundreds of Italian cheeses, only a few are used often in pasta cooking. These (either Italian imports or locally made brands) are now widely available outside of Italy.

FONTINA
Fontina is made of cow's milk and comes from the alpine areas of northwest Italy. It is ideal for melting over baked pasta dishes.

PECORINO
Pecorino cheese is made of ewe's milk. The best pecorino for grating over pasta is called *pecorino romano*, which has a sharp and pungent taste. Like parmesan, it should be bought in a wedge and grated as required.

PARMIGIANO
Parmesan is made of skimmed cow's milk and carefully aged for at least 18 months before use. If you can, try real Italian *parmigiano-reggiano* at least once; you will at least discover what parmesan should taste like. If you are buying parmesan in a good Italian grocery, a wedge will be cut from the wheel as you watch. Never buy the grated varieties; always grate it yourself as you need it.

GORGONZOLA
Gorgonzola, a speciality of northern Italy made from cow's milk, makes a wonderfully creamy pasta sauce when melted with a little butter or cream.

MOZZARELLA
Real mozzarella cheese is made from water buffalo milk, which is creamier and tastier than cow's milk. However, since it is expensive and not always easy to find outside of Italy, you will probably have to settle for mozzarella made from the milk of cows. If it is fresh and a good brand, this will be just as satisfying.

RICOTTA
Fresh ricotta has a deliciously light and delicate flavour. It forms the basis of many stuffings for filled pasta. Buy it in a good Italian grocery or specialised cheese shop. Try to avoid ricotta sold in plastic containers, which bears very little resemblance to the real thing.

HERBS AND SPICES

There are a limited number of fairly common herbs and spices that are essential in pasta cookery. It goes without saying that fresh herbs and freshly ground spices will always produce superior results to dried or powdered ones. However, fresh herbs may not always be available and in that case you should use dried ones. All herbs and spices in powdered form are to be shunned.

ORIGANO
Oregano is closely related to marjoram, but has a much stronger flavour. It is one of the few herbs that dries well, so don't worry too much if you can't get it fresh.

CAPPERI
Capers are the unopened buds of a flowering plant that grows wild on Mediterranean hillsides. They can be bought either pickled in vinegar or packed in salt. The pickled variety keeps well in the refrigerator.

PEPE NERO
Black pepper should be bought as whole peppercorns. Grind them over your sauce or dish as required.

AGLIO
Garlic is one of the basic ingredients of most pasta sauces. Always use fresh cloves, either whole or chopped. When sautéing garlic take care that it never gets past a light gold colour or it will produce a very acrid flavour that will taint the whole dish.

PEPERONCINO
Small red hot chillies are widely available throughout Italy. They keep indefinitely in an airtight jar so if you are ever in Italy, stock up on the real thing. Otherwise crushed dried chillies will be a good substitute.

ALLORO
Bay leaves are richly aromatic and are generally added whole to sauces during the cooking and removed before serving. They dry well and, stored in an airtight jar, will keep indefinitely.

NOCE MOSCATA
Buy whole nutmegs and store them in an airtight jar. Use a fine grater to grate the nutmeg as you need it.

PREZZEMOLO
Parsley is one of the basic herbs in pasta cookery.
Italian parsley is the continental flat-leaf variety
shown here. It has a different flavour from
common curly-leaf parsley and will produce
more authentic results. However since parsley
doesn't dry well, I would prefer fresh curly-
leaf parsley to dried flat-leaf.

MAGGIORANA
Marjoram's spicy aroma is
delicious with fish- and
vegetable-based sauces. It
doesn't dry well and should
always be used fresh.

BASILICO
Basil combines very well with
tomato. For full flavour, the leaves should be torn
rather than chopped and added to the sauce just
before removing from heat.

SALVIA
Sage is best fresh, but if you
are using it in its dried form,
use about half the amount
given in the recipes since it
becomes so much more
potent when dry.

ROSMARINO
Rosemary is a common herb
in Italian cooking and usually
associated with roasts. Its
finely chopped fresh leaves
will also enliven meat- and
fish-based sauces.

Utensils for Making and Cooking Pasta

Most well stocked kitchens will already have much of the basic equipment for preparing and serving pasta. If you need extra pieces they will be easy to find in kitchen-supply stores. If you can, always choose good quality equipment. It will last longer and the results will be better.

POT
Large capacity pot with a close-fitting lid.

PASTA MACHINE
This is a basic hand-cranked pasta machine. Electric versions are also available.

FRYING PAN
Heavy, shallow-sided pan in aluminum, stainless steel, or cast iron.

SAUCEPAN
Versatile pans in several sizes.

WHEEL CUTTER
To give fluted edges when cutting fresh pasta.

SAUTÉ PAN
Deep-sided pan, large enough to hold the pasta and sauce together.

CUTTING BOARD
Heavy duty board for cutting and slicing vegetables and meat.

METAL TONGS
For picking up or serving spaghetti.

COLANDER
Large metal colander for draining pasta.

WOODEN SPOON AND FORK
For stirring pasta and sauces.

CHEESE GRATER
Choose the rounded
stainless steel grater
specially designed for
parmesan and other
cheeses.

MEASURING CUP
Cup with liquid and dry
measurements.

FOOD PROCESSOR
For chopping, shredding
and puréeing ingredients
for sauces.

FOOD MILL
Hand-cranked mill for
puréeing ingredients for
filled pasta stuffings and
other ingredients for
sauces.

BAKING DISH
Large, rectangular,
ovenproof baking dish
for baked pasta.

ROLLING PIN
A pasta rolling pin is
longer and thinner than
the normal one.

SLOTTED SPOON
Used for removing
gnocchi from the pan and
for skimming broth.

TIPS FOR COOKING PASTA

TIMING
One of the most difficult things for the novice
pasta cook is knowing when the pasta is cooked.
It should be boiled until the outer layers are soft
enough to absorb the delicious sauce you have
prepared, while the inside is firm enough to pose
some resistance to the bite. This is called *al dente*.

WATER
Pasta needs lots of water to cook properly.
Allow about 4 litres (7 pints) for each 500 g
(1 pound) of pasta. Never cook even a small
amount of pasta in less than 3 litres (5 pints).

SALT
Allow at least 1 heaped tablespoon of salt for
each 500 g (1 pound) of pasta. Add the salt after
the water has come to the boil, just before
adding the pasta.

QUANTITY
As a general guideline, allow about 125 g (4 oz)
per head. If the pasta is a first course between
antipasti and the main, you may need less. If
you are just serving pasta with a salad, you may
need more.

COOKING
When the water is boiling, add all the pasta at
once. Stir with a wooden spoon so it doesn't
stick together. Cover the pot with a lid and
bring it back to the boil as soon as possible.
When the water is boiling again, leave to cook
uncovered, stirring frequently.

DRAINING
Drain the pasta in a colander as soon as it is
cooked. Don't leave it sitting in the water as it
will get mushy and overcooked.

SERVING
Pasta should be served immediately. If it is left
sitting, it will turn into a sticky lump.

Basic Sauces

This section features recipes for 14 basic sauces and suggestions for the best types of pasta with which to serve them.

Salsa al pomodoro
Simple tomato sauce

Oil-based tomato sauce goes well with all dried, hard-wheat pasta, such as spaghetti, spaghettini, penne, bucatini and fusilli. It is also good with spinach and wholewheat pasta.

Serves: 6; Preparation: 15 minutes; Cooking: 20 minutes; Level of difficulty: Simple

Put the garlic and oil in a sauté pan and cook over medium heat until the garlic is golden brown. § Add the basil and tomatoes. Season with salt and pepper, and simmer for about 15-20 minutes, or until the oil begins to separate from the tomato.

§ Cook the pasta in a large pot of salted, boiling water until *al dente*. Drain well and transfer to a heated serving dish. Toss well with the sauce and serve at once.

> VARIATIONS
> – Sauté 1 small onion, 1 carrot, 1 stalk celery, and 1 tablespoon parsley, all finely chopped, with the garlic.
> – Add ½ teaspoon crushed chillies.
> – Crumble 2 anchovy fillets into the sauce with the tomatoes.
> – Add 1 tablespoon small salted capers.

■ INGREDIENTS

- 3 cloves garlic, finely chopped
- 4 tablespoons extra-virgin olive oil
- 2 tablespoons fresh basil leaves, torn
- 600 g (1¼ lb) peeled and chopped fresh or tinned tomatoes
- salt and freshly ground black pepper
- 600 g (1¼ lb) dried pasta

Salsa di burro e pomodoro
Tomato and butter sauce

This sauce is delicious with all types of fresh pasta and gnocchi.

Serves 4; Preparation: 10 minutes; Cooking: 30 minutes; Level of difficulty: Simple

Combine the garlic and onion in a sauté pan with the butter and oil. Sauté over medium heat until the onion is transparent. § Add the tomatoes and season with salt and pepper. Simmer over medium-low heat for about 25 minutes. Add the basil just before removing from heat.

§ Cook the pasta in a large pot of salted, boiling water until *al dente*. Drain and place in a heated serving dish. Pour the sauce over the top and toss gently until well mixed. Serve hot with lots of parmesan to sprinkle over each portion.

> VARIATION
> – Stir 250 ml (8fl oz) fresh cream into the sauce after removing from heat for a *rosé* or pink sauce.

■ INGREDIENTS

- 1 clove garlic, finely chopped
- 1 small onion, very finely chopped
- 50 g (1½ oz) butter
- 1 tablespoon extra-virgin olive oil
- 400 g (12 oz) peeled and chopped fresh or tinned tomatoes
- 6 fresh basil leaves, torn
- salt and freshly ground black pepper
- 450 g (14 oz) fresh pasta

Right:
Spaghetti con salsa al pomodoro

Balsamella
Béchamel sauce

Béchamel is an essential ingredient in many filled and baked pasta dishes. It can also be used to revive leftover pasta by simply tossing the pasta and béchamel for 2-3 minutes in a pan over medium-high heat or baking together in a hot oven for about 15 minutes. Béchamel is simple and quick to make and should be used as soon as it is made.

Makes: about 300 ml (½ pint); Preparation & Cooking: 10 minutes; Level of difficulty: Simple

Heat the milk in a saucepan until it is almost boiling. § Melt the butter in a heavy-bottomed pan over low heat. Add the flour gradually and stir until smooth. § Remove from heat and add the milk a few tablespoons at a time, stirring constantly. When all the milk has been added, season with salt and return to low heat. § Cook for 3-4 minutes, or until the sauce is thick, stirring all the time. If any lumps form, beat the sauce rapidly with a fork or hand whisk until they dissolve.

■ INGREDIENTS

• 500 ml (16fl oz) milk
• 50 g (1½ oz) butter
• 4 tablespoons plain flour
• salt

Salsa di burro e parmigiano
Butter and parmesan sauce

Freshly grated parmesan tossed with hot pasta and high quality butter is always delicious. It is served with all types of dried, fresh and filled pasta, both shop-bought and homemade.

Serves: 4; Preparation & Cooking: 5 minutes; Level of difficulty: Simple

Cook the pasta in a large pot of salted, boiling water until *al dente*. Drain and transfer to a heated serving dish. § Add half the cheese and toss well until it melts creamily over the pasta. Add the butter and remaining cheese and continue to toss until the butter has melted. Serve hot.

■ INGREDIENTS

• 100 g (3½ oz) freshly grated parmesan cheese
• 50 g (1½ oz) fresh, high quality butter, chopped (not straight from the refrigerator)
• 450 g (14 oz) pasta

Salsa di burro e salvia
Butter and sage sauce

The clean, fuzzy taste of sage and butter combines well with fresh pasta and gnocchi.

Preparation & Cooking: 5 minutes; Level of difficulty: Simple

Put the butter and sage in a heavy-bottomed saucepan over low heat and leave until the butter turns light gold.
§ Cook the pasta in a large pot of salted, boiling water until *al dente*. Drain well and transfer to a heated serving dish. Pour the sauce over the pasta. Toss well, sprinkle with the parmesan and serve at once.

■ INGREDIENTS

• 75 g (2 oz) fresh, high quality butter
• 6 fresh sage leaves, torn
• 2 tablespoons freshly grated parmesan cheese
• 450 g (14 oz) fresh or filled pasta, or potato gnocchi

Right:
Preparing béchmal sauce

Ragù di carne alla bolognese
Bolognese meat sauce

The secret of a successful ragù lies in the cooking; it should be simmered over a low heat for at least 2½ hours. It can be made ahead and kept in the refrigerator for up to 3 days, or frozen. Ragù is very versatile and can be served with most dried pasta shapes, with fresh, long pasta, such as tagliatelle, with many filled pasta dishes and with potato and spinach gnocchi.

Serves: 6; Preparation: 30 minutes; Cooking: 3 hours; Level of difficulty: Simple

Combine the pancetta, onion, celery and carrot in a sauté pan with the butter and cook over medium heat until the onion is light gold in colour. § Add the beef, pork and sausage and cook until the mixture is all the same colour. Add the clove, cinnamon and pepper. Stir in the tomatoes and continue to cook over medium heat for 15 minutes. § Add the milk and season with salt. Turn the heat down to low and simmer for at least 2½ hours, stirring from time to time.

§ Cook the pasta in a large pot of salted, boiling water until *al dente*. Drain well and toss with the meat sauce. Serve hot.

■ INGREDIENTS

- 50 g (1½ oz) diced pancetta
- 1 medium onion, 1 stalk celery, 1 small carrot, all finely chopped
- 50 g (1½ oz) butter
- 250 g (8 oz) minced beef
- 60 g (2 oz) minced pork
- 60 g (2 oz) Italian pork sausage, peeled and crumbled
- 1 freshly ground clove
- pinch of cinnamon
- ¼ teaspoon freshly ground black pepper
- 400 g (14 oz) peeled and chopped fresh or tinned tomatoes
- 250 ml (8fl oz) milk
- salt
- 600 g (1¼ lb) dried, fresh or filled pasta or gnocchi

Sugo di carne veloce
Quick meat sauce

Serves: 4; Preparation: 20 minutes; Cooking: 30 minutes; Level of difficulty: Simple

Soak the mushrooms in a bowl of tepid water for 20 minutes. Rinse well and chop coarsely. § Put the onion, garlic, pancetta and oil in a sauté pan and cook over medium heat until the onion is transparent. Add the sausage and sauté for 5 more minutes. § Add the tomatoes and mushrooms, season with salt and pepper, and simmer over medium low heat for about 20 minutes, stirring frequently.

§ Cook the pasta in a large pot of salted, boiling water until *al dente*. Drain and transfer to a heated serving dish. Toss well with the sauce and serve hot.

■ INGREDIENTS

- 30 g (1 oz) dried porcini mushrooms
- 1 large onion, finely chopped
- 1 clove garlic, finely chopped
- 50 g (1½ oz) diced pancetta
- 2 tablespoons extra-virgin olive oil
- 250 g (8 oz) Italian pork sausage, peeled and crumbled
- 400g (14 oz) peeled and chopped fresh or tinned tomatoes
- salt and freshly ground black pepper
- 450 g (14 oz) dried or fresh pasta or gnocchi

Right: *Tortellini al ragù di carne alla bolognese*

Pesto alla genovese
Genoese Basil Sauce

Pesto comes from the Liguria region in northern Italy and is named for its capital city, Genoa. Traditionally it is served with trenette, a local egg-based pasta similar to fettuccine. It is also good with dried pasta, particularly the long shapes (spaghetti, spaghettini, linguine), and is delicious with potato gnocchi.

Serves: 4; Preparation: 10 minutes; Level of difficulty: Simple

Combine the basil, pine nuts, garlic, olive oil and salt in a food processor or blender and chop until smooth. Place mixture in a large serving bowl and stir in the cheeses.

§ Cook the pasta in a pot of salted, boiling water until *al dente*. Drain well and transfer to a heated serving dish. Add 2 tablespoons of the water from the pasta pot and a knob of butter. Toss vigorously with the pesto and serve hot.

> VARIATION
> – Add 1 tablespoon fresh ricotta cheese just before serving for a richer sauce.

■ INGREDIENTS

- 60 g (2 oz) fresh basil leaves
- 2 tablespoons pine nuts
- 1 clove garlic
- 8 tablespoons extra-virgin olive oil
- salt
- 2 tablespoons grated parmesan cheese
- 2 tablespoons grated pecorino cheese
- knob of butter for serving
- 450 g (14 oz) pasta

Pesto toscano
Tuscan-style pesto

This recipe is an up-dated version of one said to have been developed by the chefs of the Medici family in Florence in the 16th century. It can be served with most long and short dried pasta shapes.

Serves: 4; Preparation: 10 minutes; Level of difficulty: Simple

Put the walnuts, basil and garlic in a food processor or blender and chop to a cream. Transfer to a mixing bowl. § Remove the crust from the bread roll and soak the inside in the broth. Squeeze well and add to the walnut mixture. Add salt to taste, lemon juice and oil (you may need slightly more or slightly less oil depending on how much the walnuts absorb), and mix well.

§ Cook the pasta in a large pot of salted, boiling water until *al dente*. Drain and transfer to a heated serving dish. Toss well with the sauce and serve hot.

■ INGREDIENTS

- 20 shelled walnuts
- 30 g (1 oz) fresh basil leaves
- 1 clove garlic
- 1 medium bread roll
- 250 ml (8fl oz) meat broth (see recipe p. 34)
- salt
- juice of 1 lemon
- 2 tablespoons extra-virgin olive oil
- 450 g (14 oz) pasta

Right:
Linguine al pesto

Intingolo di funghi porcini
Italian mushroom sauce

Fresh porcini mushrooms are hard to find outside of Italy and France but they are widely available in their dried form. If you can't get fresh porcini, combine a small amount of soaked, dried porcini with fresh white mushrooms. The dried porcini have such a strong musky taste they will flavour your dish almost as well as the fresh ones. Mushroom sauce is very good with fresh pasta (tagliolini, fettuccine, tagliatelle, pappardelle) and also with long dried pasta shapes (spaghetti, bucatini, etc.). Try replacing the meat sauce in Lasagne al forno (see recipe p. 94) with 1 quantity of this sauce.

Serves: 4; Preparation: 10 minutes + time to soak the mushrooms; Cooking: 30 minutes; Level of difficulty: Simple

If you are using dried *porcini*, soak them in 250 ml (8fl oz) of warm water for about 20 minutes. Drain and squeeze out the excess water. Chop coarsely. § Put the garlic and rosemary in a large sauté pan with the butter and oil and sauté over medium heat for 4-5 minutes. Add the mushrooms and season with salt and pepper. Cover and cook over medium-low heat for about 20-25 minutes, or until the mushrooms are very tender.

§ Cook the pasta in a large pot of salted, boiling water until *al dente*. Drain and place on a heated serving dish. Cover with the sauce and toss vigorously. Serve hot.

■ INGREDIENTS

- 400 g (14 oz) coarsely chopped fresh porcini mushrooms, or 350 g (12 oz) ounces fresh white mushrooms and 60 g (2 oz) dried porcini mushrooms
- 2 cloves garlic, finely chopped
- sprig of fresh rosemary, finely chopped
- 1½ tablespoons butter
- 4 tablespoons extra-virgin olive oil
- salt and freshly ground black pepper
- 450 g (14 oz) fresh or dried pasta, or potato gnocchi

Intingolo di noci
Walnut sauce

Walnut sauce is good with fresh pasta and potato gnocchi.

Serves: 4; Preparation: 20 minutes; Cooking: 15 minutes; Level of difficulty: Simple

Roast the pine nuts in the oven at 180°C /350°F for 5-10 minutes, or until they are golden in colour. Take them out and leave to cool. § Shell the walnuts and combine in a food processor with the pine nuts, garlic, parsley and oil. Chop finely. Season with salt.

§ Cook the pasta in a large pot of salted, boiling water until *al dente*. Drain thoroughly, transfer to a heated serving bowl and toss with the sauce. Serve with lots of freshly grated parmesan for sprinkling over each portion.

■ INGREDIENTS

- 500 g (1 lb) walnuts, in their shells
- 50 g (1½ oz) pine nuts
- 2 cloves garlic
- 30 g (1 oz) parsley
- 8 tablespoons extra-virgin olive oil
- salt
- freshly grated parmesan cheese
- 450 g (14 oz) fresh pasta or potato gnocchi

Right:
Tagliolini ai funghi porcini

SUGO FINTO
False "meat" sauce

This light sauce is just as versatile as any meat sauce. Serve it hot with all pasta shapes. For an entirely vegetarian sauce, omit the pancetta and add 30 g (1 oz) ounce of dried porcini mushrooms.

Serves: 4; Preparation: 15 minutes; Cooking: 35 minutes; Level of difficulty: Simple

Put the pancetta, parsley, onion, carrots, celery and garlic in a sauté pan with the oil and butter. Cook over medium-high heat for 5 minutes. Add the tomatoes and season with salt and pepper. Simmer over medium-low heat for about 25 minutes.

§ Cook the pasta in a large pot of salted, boiling water until *al dente*. Drain well and transfer to a heated serving dish. Toss with the sauce and serve hot with lots of freshly grated parmesan on hand to sprinkle over each portion.

■ INGREDIENTS

- 50 g (1½ oz) diced pancetta
- 60 g (2 oz) finely chopped parsley
- 1 large onion, 2 carrots, 2 stalks celery, 2 cloves garlic, all finely chopped
- 2 tablespoons extra-virgin olive oil
- 50 g (1½ oz) butter
- 2 large tomatoes, peeled and chopped
- salt and freshly ground black pepper
- freshly grated parmesan cheese
- 450 g (14 oz) pasta or gnocchi

RAGÙ DI PESCE
Fish sauce

Many different sorts of fish will work in this sauce. Ask your fishmonger for fish that are suitable for making soup. Long, dried shapes, like spaghetti and spaghettini, are the classic choice of pasta. Short, dried pasta shapes, such as penne and maccheroni, are also a good match.

Serves: 4; Preparation: 15 minutes; Cooking: 50 minutes; Level of difficulty: Medium

Place the fish in a pot with abundant water and the rosemary and bring to the boil. Cook for 15 minutes over medium-low heat. Take the fish out, remove the skin and bones, and crumble the cooked meat. Strain the liquid and discard the rosemary leaves. § Sauté the onion and garlic in a large sauté pan with the oil until light gold in colour. Add the fish meat and 750 ml (24fl oz) of the broth in which it was cooked. Season with salt and pepper and simmer over low heat for about 30-35 minutes.

§ Cook the pasta in a large pot of salted, boiling water until *al dente*. Drain well and transfer to the sauté pan with the fish sauce. Add the parsley and toss well. Serve immediately.

■ INGREDIENTS

- 600-700 g (1¼-1½ lb) assorted fresh fish, such as hake, sea bass, sea bream and red snapper, gutted
- 2 tablespoons fresh rosemary leaves
- 1 medium onion, finely chopped
- 1 clove garlic, finely chopped
- 8 tablespoons extra-virgin olive oil
- salt and freshly ground black pepper
- 1 tablespoon finely chopped parsley
- 450 g (14 oz) dried pasta

Right:
Maccheroni al ragù di pesce

Brodo di carne
Meat broth

Homemade meat broth is used as the basis for many soups, to serve tortellini and agnolotti in brodo, and to flavour a number of other pasta dishes. It can be made ahead of time and kept in the refrigerator for up to 3 days or frozen. Don't worry too much if you don't have one or two of the vegetables, the broth will still be good.

Makes: about 2 litres (3½ pints); Preparation: 15 minutes; Cooking: 3 hours; Level of difficulty: Simple

Put the meat, vegetables and salt and pepper to taste in a large pot with the water. Cover and bring to the boil over medium heat. Simmer over low heat for 3 hours. Occasionally, skim the scum off the top so that the broth will be light and fresh to taste. § Remove from heat and leave to cool. When the broth is cool, a layer of fat will form on the top. This should be skimmed off.

§ To make *Minestrina in brodo di carne*, allow about 250 ml (8fl oz) of broth and about 60 g (2 oz) of pasta per person. Put the broth in a saucepan or pot, add the pasta, and simmer until the pasta is *al dente*. Serve hot. Sprinkle each portion with freshly grated parmesan.

> VARIATION
> – To make chicken broth, replace the beef with chicken.

■ INGREDIENTS

- 1 kg (2 lb) beef
- 1 kg (2 lb) meat bones
- 1 carrot
- 1 onion
- 1 stalk celery
- 1 whole clove
- 1 bay leaf
- 1 clove garlic
- 5 sprigs parsley
- 1 leek
- 1 ripe tomato
- 2 litres (3½ pints) water
- salt and freshly ground black pepper
- freshly grated parmesan cheese

Brodo di pesce
Fish broth

Fish broth makes a delicious change from meat broth as the basis for minestrine.

Makes: about 1 litre (1¾ pints); Preparation: 15 minutes; Cooking: 1¼ hours; Level of difficulty: Simple

Put the fish and vegetables in a large pot with the water. Bring to a boil. Cover and leave to simmer over low heat for 1 hour. Season with salt and simmer for 15 more minutes.

§ Serve hot with small, soup pasta shapes following the recipe above for *Minestrina in brodo*, or with *Ravioli di pesce* (see recipe p. 90).

■ INGREDIENTS

- 1½ litres (2¼ pints) water
- 600 g (1¼ lb) assorted fresh fish, such as hake, sea bass, sea bream and red snapper, cleaned and gutted
- 2 stalks celery
- 1 carrot
- 1 medium onion
- 2 cloves garlic
- 2 ripe tomatoes, peeled and chopped
- 1 tablespoon parsley
- salt

Right:
Minestrina in brodo

DRIED PASTA

By dried pasta we mean shop-bought pasta
made from hard-wheat flour and water.
It includes classics such as spaghetti,
penne, fusilli and maccheroni.

Spaghettini con aglio olio e peperoncino
Spaghettini with garlic, oil and chillies

The sauce is very quick to make and should be used immediately, so begin by cooking the spaghettini in a large pot of salted, boiling water.

Serves: 4; Preparation: 3 minutes; Cooking: 10 minutes; Level of difficulty: Simple

While the pasta is cooking, combine the oil, garlic and chillies in a small frying pan and cook over low heat until the garlic begins to change colour. Remove from heat at once, taking care not to burn the garlic because it will give the sauce a bitter flavour. Add the parsley and salt to taste. § Drain the pasta when *al dente* and place in a heated serving dish. Pour the sauce over the pasta and toss vigorously. Serve immediately.

■ INGREDIENTS

- 8 tablespoons extra-virgin olive oil
- 2 cloves garlic, finely chopped
- ¼-½ teaspoon crushed chillies
- 1 tablespoon finely chopped parsley
- salt
- 450 g (14 oz) spaghettini

Wine: a dry white (Trebbiano)

Spaghetti alla carbonara
Spaghetti with eggs and pancetta

La carbonara is a classic Roman sauce. According to some, it was first made during the last days of World War II as American troops advanced up the Italian peninsula bringing supplies of eggs and bacon which they asked the Italians to make into a sauce. Try replacing the pancetta with bacon and decide for yourself about the historical value of this theory.

Serves: 4; Preparation: 5 minutes; Cooking: 15 minutes; Level of difficulty: Simple

Chop the cloves of garlic in half. Combine the oil, garlic and pancetta in a sauté pan and cook over medium heat until the pancetta is golden brown but not crisp. Remove the pan from the heat and take out the pieces of garlic. § In a mixing bowl lightly beat the eggs, parmesan, pecorino and salt until smooth. Set aside. § Cook the spaghetti in a large pot of salted, boiling water until *al dente*. Drain and place in a large, heated serving dish. Add the egg mixture and toss. § Return the sauté pan with the pancetta to high heat for 1 minute. Pour the hot oil and pancetta over the pasta and egg, and toss vigorously. Grind a generous amount of black pepper over the top and serve immediately.

■ INGREDIENTS

- 2 cloves garlic
- 2 tablespoons extra-virgin olive oil
- 100 g (3½ oz) diced pancetta
- 3 fresh eggs
- 2 tablespoons freshly grated parmesan cheese
- 2 tablespoons freshly grated pecorino cheese
- salt and freshly ground black pepper
- 450 g (14 oz) spaghetti

Wine: a light, young red (Vino Novello)

Right:
Spaghetti alla carbonara

Bucatini con capperi e olive
Bucatini with capers and black olives

This simple dish is from Lazio, the region around Rome. If the olives and capers are very salty, you may not need to add any extra salt. Taste the sauce before putting any in.

Serves: 4; Preparation: 10 minutes; Cooking: 15 minutes; Level of difficulty: Simple

Combine the oil, garlic and parsley in a large sauté pan and cook over medium heat until the garlic starts to change colour. Stir the olives and capers into the sauce and cook over low heat for 2-3 minutes. § Cook the bucatini in a large pot of salted, boiling water until *al dente*. Drain and transfer to the sauté pan. Toss with the capers and olives over medium-hot heat for 2 minutes. Place in a heated serving dish and sprinkle with pecorino. Serve hot.

> VARIATION
> – Replace half the pecorino with parmesan cheese. This will make the sauce slightly "sweeter."

■ INGREDIENTS

- 2 tablespoons extra-virgin olive oil
- 1 clove garlic, finely chopped
- 2 tablespoons finely chopped parsley
- 100 g (3½ oz) pitted and coarsely chopped black olives
- 2 tablespoons capers
- salt (optional)
- 4 tablespoons freshly grated pecorino cheese
- 450 g (14 oz) bucatini

Wine: a dry red (Nebbiolo)

Spaghettini alla puttanesca
Spaghettini with spicy tomato sauce

This sauce is a speciality of the beautiful island of Ischia, off the coast of Naples in southern Italy.

Serves: 4; Preparation: 10 minutes; Cooking: 25-30 minutes; Level of difficulty: Simple

Put the garlic and chillies in a sauté pan with the oil. Sauté over medium heat until the garlic begins to change colour. Add the tomatoes, capers and olives, and cook for 5 minutes. § Stir the anchovy fillets into the sauce. Season with salt and pepper and simmer over medium heat for 15-20 minutes, or until the oil and tomatoes begin to separate. § Cook the spaghettini in a large pot of salted, boiling water until *al dente*. Drain and transfer to a heated serving dish. Pour the sauce over the top and toss vigorously. Serve hot.

■ INGREDIENTS

- 1 clove garlic, finely chopped
- ¼ teaspoon crushed chillies
- 2 tablespoons extra-virgin olive oil
- 400 g (12 oz) peeled and chopped fresh or tinned tomatoes
- 4 anchovy fillets, lightly crushed with a fork
- 100 g (3½ oz) pitted and coarsely chopped black olives
- 1 tablespoon capers
- salt and freshly ground black pepper
- 450 g (14 oz) spaghettini

Wine: a dry white (Vernaccia)

Right: *Bucatini all'amatriciana*

■ INGREDIENTS

- 100 g (3½ oz) diced pancetta
- 1 tablespoon extra-virgin olive oil
- 1 small onion, finely chopped
- 400 g (14 oz) peeled and chopped fresh tomatoes
- ½ teaspoon crushed chillies
- salt
- 4 tablespoons freshly grated pecorino cheese
- 450 g (14 oz) bucatini

BUCATINI ALL'AMATRICIANA
Bucatini with pancetta and spicy tomato sauce

Serves: 4; Preparation: 5 minutes; Cooking: 30 minutes; Level of difficulty: Simple

Sauté the pancetta in a sauté pan with the oil for 2-3 minutes. Add the onion and continue cooking until it becomes transparent. Stir in the tomatoes and chillies. Season with salt and cook over medium-low heat for about 20 minutes, or until the tomatoes have separated from the oil. § Cook the bucatini in a large pot of salted, boiling water until *al dente*. Drain well and transfer to a heated serving bowl. Toss with the sauce and pecorino and serve immediately.

INGREDIENTS

- 6 medium-size ripe tomatoes
- 1 clove garlic, finely chopped
- 4 tablespoons extra-virgin olive oil
- juice of 1 lemon
- salt and freshly ground black pepper
- 100 g (3½ oz) fresh mozzarella, diced into 1 cm (½ in) cubes
- 6 fresh basil leaves, torn
- 450 g (14 oz) penne rigate (plain, wholewheat or coloured)

Wine: a light, dry white (Pinot grigio)

PENNE CON SALSA DI POMODORO FRESCO
Penne with fresh tomatoes, garlic and mozzarella cheese

This dish is a treat in the summer when ripe, tasty tomatoes are plentiful. It is quick to make and can be varied in a number of ways, according to what you have in the pantry. The sauce is good with many different types of pasta. Try it with spaghetti, fusilli or cavatappi.

Serves: 4; Preparation: 5 minutes; Cooking: 10 minutes; Level of difficulty: Simple

Peel the tomatoes with a swivel-bladed peeler. Chop them into bite-sized chunks and drain off any extra liquid. Place them in a serving bowl. Add the garlic, 3 tablespoons of the oil and lemon juice. Season with salt and pepper. § Cook the penne in a large pot of salted, boiling water until *al dente*. Drain well and toss with the remaining oil. § When the pasta is cool, transfer to the bowl with the tomato sauce and toss well. Sprinkle the mozzarella and basil over the top and serve.

> VARIATIONS
> – Add 100 g (3½ oz) black olives.
> – Add 1 tablespoon capers.
> – Add ½ teaspoon crushed chillies.
> – Add 2 tablespoons chopped shallots.

INGREDIENTS

- 1 small onion, finely chopped
- 4 tablespoons extra-virgin olive oil
- juice of 2 lemons
- salt and freshly ground black pepper
- 4 tablespoons freshly grated parmesan cheese
- 350 g (11 oz) capelli d'angelo

Wine: a dry white (Frascati)

Left:
Capelli d'angelo olio e limone

CAPELLI D'ANGELO OLIO E LIMONE
Capelli d'angelo with oil and lemon sauce

Serves: 4; Preparation: 3 minutes; Cooking: 5 minutes; Level of difficulty: Simple

Combine the onion and oil in a large sauté pan. Cook over medium heat until the onion turns golden in colour. § Cook the capelli d'angelo in a large pot of salted, boiling water until *al dente*. Drain well and transfer to the pan with the onion. Toss the pasta briefly with the onion over medium heat and transfer to a large, heated serving dish. Add the lemon juice, salt, pepper and parmesan. Toss well and serve immediately.

> VARIATION
> – For a creamier sauce, toss a raw egg yolk together with the lemon juice and parmesan.

Penne all'arrabbiata
Penne with "angry" tomato sauce

Serves: 4; Preparation: 15 minutes; Cooking: 30 minutes; Level of difficulty: Simple

Put the pancetta, garlic, celery and onion in a large sauté pan with the oil and cook until lightly browned. Add the tomatoes, mint, basil, parsley and chillies. Season with salt and pepper. § Simmer over medium-low heat for about 20 minutes or until the tomatoes and oil begin to separate. § Cook the penne in a large pot of salted, boiling water until *al dente*. Drain and toss with the sauce in the pan over high heat for 2-3 minutes. Transfer to a heated serving dish and serve hot.

VARIATIONS
- Double the amount of chillies for a really fiery dish.
- Add 2 tablespoons grated pecorino cheese just before serving.

■ INGREDIENTS

- 50 g (1½ oz) diced pancetta
- 3 cloves garlic, ½ celery stalk, 1 small onion, all finely chopped
- 2 tablespoons extra-virgin olive oil
- 500 g (1 lb) peeled and chopped fresh or tinned tomatoes
- 4 fresh mint leaves, torn
- 4 fresh basil leaves, torn
- 2 tablespoons finely chopped parsley
- ½ teaspoon crushed chillies
- salt and freshly ground black pepper
- 450 g (14 oz) penne rigate

Wine: a dry red (Montepulciano)

Penne con i carciofi
Penne with artichokes

Serves: 4; Preparation: 30 minutes; Cooking: 30 minutes; Level of difficulty: Simple

Wash the artichokes and remove all but the pale inner leaves by pulling the outer ones down and snapping them off. Cut off the stalk and the top third of the remaining leaves. Remove any tough pieces of leaves at the base with a sharp knife. Cut the artichokes in half lengthwise and scrape the fuzzy choke away with the knife. Cut each artichoke half into thin slices lengthwise and place in a bowl of cold water with the lemon juice. Soak for 20 minutes. Remove and pat dry with kitchen paper. § Put the oil and garlic in a large sauté pan and cook until the garlic begins to change colour. Add the artichokes and cook over medium-low heat for about 25 minutes, or until the artichokes are very tender. Add water if all the oil has been absorbed. Season with salt and pepper. § Cook the penne in a large pot of salted, boiling water until *al dente*. Drain well and toss with the artichoke sauce over high heat for 2-3 minutes. Sprinkle with the parsley and pecorino. Serve hot.

■ INGREDIENTS

- 6 artichokes
- juice of 1 lemon
- 4 tablespoons extra-virgin olive oil
- 2 cloves garlic, finely chopped
- salt and freshly ground black pepper
- 2 tablespoons finely chopped parsley
- 3 tablespoons freshly grated pecorino cheese
- 450 g (14 oz) penne lisce or rigate

Wine: a dry white (Orvieto)

Right:
Penne con i carciofi

■ INGREDIENTS

- 125 ml (4fl oz) milk
- 200 g (6½ oz) fresh
  ricotta cheese
- ½ tablespoon sugar
- ½ teaspoon cinnamon
- salt
- white pepper
- 450 g (14 oz) penne lisce
  or rigate

*Wine: a light, dry white
(Verdicchio)*

PENNE CON RICOTTA
Penne with ricotta cheese

This is a classic southern Italian recipe. It is very simple and everything depends on the quality and freshness of the ricotta. Buy it loose from a speciality cheese shop or a good Italian grocery. This sauce is also good with homemade fettuccine (see recipe p. 120-122).

Serves: 4; Preparation: 5 minutes; Cooking: 10 minutes; Level of difficulty: Simple

Warm the milk and place in a bowl with the ricotta, sugar, cinnamon and a pinch of salt and white pepper. Mix with a fork to form a smooth, creamy sauce. § Cook the penne in a large pot of salted, boiling water until *al dente*. Drain well and place in a heated serving bowl. Toss with the sauce and serve.

Festonati con salsicce e broccoli
Festonati with Italian sausages and broccoli

Serves: 4; Preparation: 10 minutes; Cooking: 30 minutes; Level of difficulty: Simple

Divide the broccoli into bite-sized florets. Dice the stems into similar sized cubes. Plunge the florets and stems into a large pot of salted, boiling water and cook for about 5 minutes, or until tender-crunchy. Drain well and set aside. § Place the oil in a large sauté pan with the garlic and parsley over medium heat. When the garlic begins to change colour, add the sausages and tomato paste. Cook over medium heat for 5 minutes. Add the broccoli, season with salt and pepper and cook for 10-15 minutes. § Cook the festonati in a large pot of salted, boiling water until *al dente*. Drain and toss with the sauce. Sprinkle with pecorino and serve hot.

> VARIATION
> – Add a thinly sliced leek to the garlic and parsley. It will take 3-4 minutes extra to cook.

INGREDIENTS
- 250 g (8 oz) broccoli
- 2 tablespoons extra-virgin olive oil
- 2 cloves garlic, finely chopped
- 1 tablespoon finely chopped parsley
- 200 g (6½ oz) Italian pork sausages, skinned and crumbled
- 1 tablespoon tomato paste
- salt and freshly ground black pepper
- 3 tablespoons freshly grated pecorino cheese
- 450 g (14 oz) festonati

Wine: a young, dry red (Vino Novello)

Rigatoni con gli zucchini
Rigatoni with courgettes

Serves: 4; Preparation: 10 minutes; Cooking: 25 minutes; Level of difficulty: Simple

Heat the butter and oil together in a sauté pan. Cut the clove of garlic in half, add to the pan, and cook until it starts to change colour. Remove the garlic pieces and add the courgettes. Sauté over a high heat until they begin to turn golden brown. § Turn the heat down, cover the pan with a lid, and simmer until the courgettes are tender. Season with salt and pepper. § Cook the rigatoni in a large pot of salted, boiling water until *al dente*. Drain and transfer to a heated serving dish. Add the courgettes, parsley and parmesan, and toss well. Serve hot.

> VARIATIONS
> – Add ½ teaspoon crushed chillies for a spicy dish.
> – If you prefer crunchy vegetables, add the courgettes to the pasta as soon as they are golden brown, without simmering until tender.

INGREDIENTS
- 2 tablespoons butter
- 2 tablespoons extra-virgin olive oil
- 1 clove garlic
- 3-4 courgettes (zucchini), sliced into thin wheels
- salt and freshly ground black pepper
- 2 tablespoons finely chopped parsley
- 3 tablespoons freshly grated parmesan cheese
- 450 g (14 oz) rigatoni

Wine: a dry white (Orvieto Classico)

Right:
Festonati con salsicce e broccoli

Spaghetti allo scoglio
Spaghetti with shellfish sauce

Serves: 4: Preparation: 15 minutes; Cooking: 35 minutes; Level of difficulty: Simple

Scrub the mussels and clams and soak them in cold water for 5 minutes. § Put half the garlic and 2 tablespoons of the oil in a sauté pan. Cook over medium heat until the garlic begins to change colour. Add the tomatoes, basil, half the parsley and the vinegar. Season with salt and pepper and leave to simmer for about 20 minutes or until the sauce has reduced. § Put the remaining oil, garlic, parsley and slices of lemon in another sauté pan. Cook over medium heat until the garlic begins to change colour. Add the mussels and clams and turn up the heat. When all the shellfish are open, add them (with their liquid) to the pan with the tomato sauce. Simmer for 2-3 minutes, or until the sauce has reduced. § Cook the spaghetti in a large pot of salted, boiling water until *al dente*. Drain and transfer to a heated serving dish. Pour the sauce over the top and toss well. Serve immediately.

VARIATIONS
- Add ½ teaspoon crushed chillies to the garlic and oil.
- Add a crushed bay leaf to the oil and lemon sauce.

■ INGREDIENTS

- 500 g (1 lb) mussels
- 500 g (1 lb) clams
- 2 cloves garlic, finely chopped
- 4 tablespoons extra-virgin olive oil
- 500 g (1 lb) peeled and chopped fresh tomatoes
- 6 fresh basil leaves, torn
- 6 tablespoons finely chopped parsley
- 1 teaspoon vinegar
- salt and freshly ground black pepper
- 3 slices of lemon
- 450 g (14 oz) spaghetti

Wine: a light, dry white (Vermentino)

Spaghetti alle vongole
Spaghetti with clams

Serves: 4; Preparation: 10 minutes; Cooking: 30 minutes; Level of difficulty: Simple

Scrub the clams thoroughly and soak in cold water for 5 minutes. § Put 2 tablespoons of the oil in a large sauté pan and warm over medium heat. Add the clams and white wine, and cook until all the clams are open. Remove the clams, discarding any that have not opened, and set aside. Put the clam liquid in a bowl and set aside. § Combine the remaining oil and garlic in the same pan and cook until the garlic begins to change colour. Add the tomatoes and cook over medium heat for about 5 minutes. Pour in the clam liquid. Season with salt and pepper. Cook for 15 more minutes, or until the sauce becomes thick. Add the clams and parsley, and continue cooking for 2-3 minutes. § Cook the spaghetti in a large pot of salted, boiling water until *al dente*. Drain and transfer to the sauté pan with the sauce. Toss for 1-2 minutes over medium-hot heat. Serve immediately.

■ INGREDIENTS

- 750 g (1½ lb) clams
- 4 tablespoons extra-virgin olive oil
- 4 tablespoons dry white wine
- 2 cloves garlic, finely chopped
- 4 ripe tomatoes, peeled and chopped
- salt and freshly ground black pepper
- 1 tablespoon finely chopped parsley
- 450 g (14 oz) spaghetti

Wine: a dry white (Tocai)

Right:
Spaghetti alle vongole

Ingredients

- 50 g (1½ oz) butter
- 4 tablespoons vodka
- juice of 1 lemon
- 60g (2oz) smoked salmon
- 2 teaspoons caviar
- 2 tablespoons fresh cream
- salt and freshly ground black pepper
- 450 g (14 oz) farfalle

Wine: a dry white (Soave)

FARFALLE AL SALMONE E VODKA
Farfalle with smoked salmon and vodka sauce

Serves: 4; Preparation: 5 minutes; Cooking: 15 minutes; Level of difficulty: Simple

Put the butter, vodka and lemon juice in a heavy-bottomed pan. Cook over low heat until the vodka has evaporated. § Crumble the smoked salmon with a fork. Add with the caviar to the pan. Cook over medium-low heat for 2-3 minutes. Add the cream and salt and pepper to taste. Remove from heat. § Cook the farfalle in a large pot of salted, boiling water until *al dente*. Drain well and transfer to the pan with the salmon sauce. Toss well over medium heat and serve immediately.

Spaghetti con le seppie
Spaghetti with cuttlefish

INGREDIENTS

- 6 cuttlefish
- 1 medium onion
- 1 clove garlic, finely chopped
- 4 tablespoons extra-virgin olive oil
- 200 g (6½ oz) peeled and chopped fresh or tinned tomatoes
- salt and freshly ground black pepper
- 450 g (14 oz) spaghetti

Wine: a dry white

Serves 4; Preparation: 20 minutes; Cooking: about 1 hour; Level of difficulty: Medium

Rinse the cuttlefish thoroughly in cold water. To clean, cut each cuttlefish lengthwise and remove the internal bone and the stomach. Take care not to break the internal ink sac. Set the sacs aside. Cut the cuttlefish crosswise into thin half circles. § Combine the onion and garlic with the oil in a large sauté pan and cook over medium heat until they begin to change colour. Add the cuttlefish and tomatoes. Season with salt and pepper. Turn the heat down low, cover, and simmer for about 45 minutes, or until the cuttlefish are tender. § Add the ink and stir over medium heat for 2-3 minutes. § Cook the spaghetti in a large pot of salted, boiling water until *al dente*. Drain well and transfer to a heated serving dish. Toss vigorously with the sauce and serve hot.

Linguine con le fave
Linguine with broad beans and fresh rosemary

INGREDIENTS

- 1 kg (2 lb) broad beans in their pods
- 1 clove garlic
- 2 sprigs fresh rosemary
- 50 g (1½ oz) butter
- 2 tablespoons extra-virgin olive oil
- 1 medium onion, finely chopped
- 250 ml (8fl oz) meat broth (see recipe p. 34)
- salt and freshly ground black pepper
- 4 tablespoons freshly grated parmesan cheese
- 450 g (14 oz) linguine

Wine: a light, dry white (Verdicchio)

If fresh broad beans are out of season, use 1-1¼ pounds of frozen ones. This sauce is also good with many short pasta shapes, such as conchiglie, lumaconi or rigatoni.

Serves: 4; Preparation: 15 minutes; Cooking: about 30 minutes; Level of difficulty: Simple

Pod the beans and set aside in a bowl of cold water. § Cut the clove of garlic in two and combine with the rosemary, half the butter and the oil in a sauté pan. Sauté over medium heat until the garlic begins to change colour. Remove the garlic and rosemary, making sure that none of the leaves remain in the sauce. Lower heat to medium, add the onion, and sauté until transparent. § Drain the broad beans and add with the broth to the sauté pan. Season with salt and pepper. Continue to cook over medium-low heat for about 20 minutes or until the beans are tender, stirring from time to time. § Cook the linguine in a large pot of salted, boiling water until *al dente*. Drain and place in a heated serving dish. Pour the sauce over the pasta and toss with the parmesan and the remaining butter until well mixed. Serve hot.

Right:
Linguine con le fave

■ INGREDIENTS

- 4 tablespoons extra-virgin olive oil
- 400 g (13 oz) peeled and chopped fresh or tinned tomatoes
- 1 teaspoon oregano
- salt and freshly ground black pepper
- 100 g (3½ oz) diced mozzarella cheese
- 3 tablespoons freshly grated pecorino cheese
- 450 g (14 oz) fusilli

Wine: a dry white
(Greco di Tufo)

■ INGREDIENTS

- 4 tablespoons extra-virgin olive oil
- 1 small green, 1 small yellow, and 1 small red pepper
- 1 large onion, finely chopped
- 1 clove garlic, finely chopped
- 200 g (6½ oz) peeled and chopped fresh or tinned tomatoes
- 6 basil leaves, torn
- 2 tablespoons boiling water
- salt and freshly ground black pepper
- 2 tablespoons vinegar
- 4 anchovy fillets
- 450 g (14 oz) maccheroni

Wine: a dry red

Left:
Fusilli alla vesuviana

Fusilli alla vesuviana
Fusilli with tomato and mozzarella cheese

This dish comes from Campania, the region of which Naples is the capital city. The volcano Vesuvius towers above the Bay of Naples and has given its name to this dish invented in its shadows.

Serves: 4; Preparation: 10 minutes; Cooking: 20 minutes; Level of difficulty: Simple

Place the oil in a sauté pan over medium heat. Add the tomatoes, oregano, salt and pepper, and cook for about 15 minutes, stirring from time to time. When the tomatoes begin to separate from the oil, remove from heat. § Cook the fusilli in a large pot of salted, boiling water until *al dente*. Drain well and place in a heated serving dish. Add the mozzarella and pecorino and toss vigorously. Serve immediately.

Maccheroni con i peperoni
Maccheroni with peppers

Serves: 4; Preparation: 10 minutes; Cooking: 40 minutes; Level of difficulty: Simple

Cut the peppers in half lengthwise. Remove stalks, seeds and membrane, and cut crosswise into strips about ½ cm (¼ in) in width. § Combine oil, peppers, onion and garlic in a large sauté pan and cook until the garlic turns golden brown. Add the tomatoes, basil and boiling water. Season with salt and pepper. § Simmer over medium heat for 20-25 minutes or until the peppers are tender, stirring from time to time. § Stir in the vinegar and anchovies, and cook over high heat for 2-3 minutes until the vinegar evaporates. Remove from heat. § Cook the maccheroni in a large pot of salted, boiling water until *al dente*. Drain well and transfer to a heated serving dish. Pour the sauce over the top and toss well. Serve hot.

VARIATION
– For a more filling dish, place the cooked pasta in a baking dish, pour the sauce over the top and mix well. Spread 150 g (5 oz) thinly sliced mozzarella cheese on top and bake in preheated oven at 180° C /350° F for 10 minutes or until the mozzarella turns golden brown.

Spaghettini al tonno
Spaghettini with tuna and tomato sauce

Ideally you should use caciocavallo cheese, but if this is not available, use a tasty pecorino instead. Don't use parmesan in this recipe.

Serves: 4; Preparation: 15 minutes; Cooking: 35 minutes; Level of difficulty: Simple

Put the oil, garlic, onion and anchovy to cook in a large sauté pan over a medium-high heat for 3-4 minutes. Add the tomatoes and simmer over medium heat for 25 minutes, stirring from time to time. § Stir in the tuna, oregano and black pepper. Taste the sauce and, if necessary, add salt. Simmer over medium heat for another 5 minutes. § Cook the spaghettini in a large pot of salted, boiling water until *al dente*. Drain well and transfer to a heated serving dish. Toss with the sauce and caciocavallo (or pecorino). Serve hot.

■ INGREDIENTS

• 6 tablespoons extra-virgin olive oil
• 2 cloves garlic, finely chopped
• 1 medium onion, finely chopped
• 1 anchovy fillet
• 300 g (9½ oz) peeled and chopped fresh or tinned tomatoes
• 100 g (3½ oz) tuna fish
• ½ teaspoon dried oregano
• 50 g (1½ oz) freshly grated caciocavallo cheese
• salt and freshly ground black pepper
• 450 g (14 oz) spaghettini

Wine: a light, dry white (Galestro)

Bucatoni con le cipolle
Bucatoni with onion sauce

Serves: 4; Preparation: 5 minutes; Cooking: 50 minutes; Level of difficulty: Simple

Put the onions in a sauté pan with the butter and oil. Sauté over medium heat until they begin to change colour. Add salt and pepper to taste. § Turn the heat down to low, cover, and simmer for about 40 minutes, or until the onions are very soft. § Uncover and add the wine. Turn the heat up to medium and stir while the wine evaporates. Remove from heat. § Break the thick bucatoni noodles in half and cook in a large pot of salted, boiling water until they are *al dente*. Drain well and transfer to a heated serving dish. Pour the onion sauce over the top. Add the parsley and parmesan, and toss vigorously until the sauce and pasta are well mixed. Serve hot.

■ INGREDIENTS

• 3 large onions, sliced in thin rings
• 50 g (1½ oz) butter
• 2 tablespoons extra-virgin olive oil
• salt and freshly ground black pepper
• 125 ml (4fl oz) dry white wine
• 2 tablespoons finely chopped parsley
• 6 tablespoons freshly grated parmesan cheese
• 450 g (14 oz) bucatoni

Wine: a dry white (Orvieto)

Right:
Farfalle con piselli e prosciutto

INGREDIENTS

- 100 g (3½ oz) peas
- 50 g (1½ oz) butter
- 100 g (3½ oz) boiled ham, diced into small cubes
- 2 tablespoons fresh cream
- 1 tablespoon finely chopped parsley
- salt and freshly ground black pepper
- 2 tablespoons freshly grated parmesan cheese
- 450 g (14 oz) farfalle

Farfalle con piselli e prosciutto
Farfalle with peas and ham

Serves: 4; Preparation: 5 minutes; Cooking: 20 minutes; Level of difficulty: Simple

Boil the peas in salted water until half cooked. § Combine the peas, butter and ham in a large sauté pan. Cook over medium-low heat for 10 minutes. Stir in 1 tablespoon of the cream and continue cooking until the sauce becomes thick. Add the parsley, and salt and pepper to taste. § Cook the farfalle in a large pot of salted, boiling water until *al dente*. Drain well and transfer to the sauté pan with the sauce. Add the remaining cream and parmesan. Toss well and serve hot.

Lumaconi all'ortolana
Lumaconi with vegetables

Serves: 4; Preparation: 10 minutes; Cooking: 35 minutes; Level of difficulty: Simple

Chop the onion coarsely. Peel the aubergine and dice it and the courgette into bite-sized cubes. Remove the stalks and cores from the peppers and chop into small squares. § Put the onion in a large sauté pan with the oil and cook over medium heat until it becomes transparent. Add the aubergine, peppers and courgettes. Sauté the vegetables for 7-8 minutes. Add the tomatoes, crushed chillies and salt to taste. Cook for 20 minutes. § Cook the lumaconi in a large pot of salted, boiling water until *al dente*. Drain and add to the sauté pan with the vegetables. Toss over high heat for 2-3 minutes until well mixed. Add the basil and parmesan. Transfer to a heated serving dish and serve hot.

■ INGREDIENTS

- 1 small onion
- 1 small aubergine (eggplant)
- 1 medium courgette (zucchini)
- 1 small green, 1 small yellow, 1 small red pepper
- 4 tablespoons extra-virgin olive oil
- 400 g (12 oz) peeled and chopped fresh tomatoes
- ½ teaspoon crushed chillies
- salt
- 5-6 basil leaves, torn
- 2 tablespoons freshly grated parmesan cheese
- 450 g (14 oz) lumaconi

Wine: a dry white (Bianco San Severo)

Conchiglie al cavolfiore
Conchiglie with cauliflower, garlic and chillies

Serves: 4; Preparation: 5 minutes; Cooking: 25 minutes; Level of difficulty: Simple

Divide the cauliflower into bite-sized florets and dice the stalk into small cubes. Cook in boiling water until half cooked (about 7 minutes). Drain and set aside. § Combine the oil, butter and onion in a large sauté pan and cook until the onion is transparent. Add the garlic and crushed chillies and sauté until the garlic begins to change colour. § Add the cauliflower pieces and cook over medium-low heat for 8-10 more minutes, or until the cauliflower is tender. Season with salt and pepper. § Cook the conchiglie in a large pot of salted, boiling water until *al dente*. Drain well and transfer to the sauté pan. Toss the pasta and sauce together over medium heat for 2-3 minutes. Serve hot.

■ INGREDIENTS

- 1 medium cauliflower
- 2 tablespoons extra-virgin olive oil
- 2 tablespoons butter
- 1 small onion
- 3 cloves garlic, finely chopped
- ½ teaspoon crushed chillies
- salt and freshly ground black pepper
- 450 g (14 oz) conchiglie

Wine: a light, dry white (Cortese)

VARIATIONS
- Replace the cauliflower with green broccoli.
- Add 4 peeled tomatoes to the sauté pan with the cauliflower pieces.

Right: *Conchiglie al cavolfiore* and *Lumaconi all'ortolana*

Malloreddus
Malloreddus with Italian sausages and pecorino cheese

Malloreddus ("little bulls"), or gnocchi sardi *as they are also known, are a speciality of
the island of Sardinia. They are quite unlike the other dried pasta in this section, being made of
bran flour and saffron. Malloreddus can be made fresh at home, but it is a difficult and
time-consuming task and good commercial varieties are now available.*

Serves: 4; Preparation: 5 minutes; Cooking: 30 minutes; Level of difficulty: Simple

Combine the oil, sausages, onion, garlic and basil in a sauté pan and cook
over medium heat until the onion turns golden brown. Add the tomatoes
and salt and pepper to taste. Simmer for 15-20 minutes or until the sauce
has reduced. § Cook the malloreddus in a large pot of salted, boiling water
until *al dente*. Drain well and transfer to a heated serving dish. § Add the
sauce and pecorino, and toss. Serve hot with lots of pecorino or parmesan
on hand to sprinkle over each portion.

Spaghetti alla Norma
Spaghetti with fried aubergine

Pasta alla Norma *is a classic Sicilian dish. Debate rages about the origins of the name. Some
say that it is named after Bellini's famous opera. Others maintain that it simply means la
norma, or something that happens often. It may also derive from the Catanese dialect, in
which norma means "the very best."*

Serves: 4; Preparation: 1½ hours; Cooking: 40 minutes; Level of difficulty: Simple

Cut the aubergines into ½ cm (¼ in) slices, sprinkle with salt and place on a
slanted cutting board, so that the bitter liquid they produce can run off.
This will take about 1 hour. § Put the olive oil and garlic in a sauté pan over
medium heat and cook until the garlic turns gold. Add the tomatoes, basil,
and salt and pepper to taste. Cook over medium-low heat for about 20
minutes, or until the oil and tomatoes begin to separate. § Run the
aubergine under cold water and pat dry with paper towels. Put 3 cm (1¼ in)
of vegetable oil in a large sauté pan. When the oil is hot, add as many slices
of aubergine as will fit without overlapping. Fry to golden brown on both
sides and place on paper towels. When all the aubergine is fried, chop into
large squares. § Cook the spaghetti in a large pot of salted, boiling water
until *al dente*. Drain well and transfer to a heated serving dish. Toss with the
tomato sauce and fried aubergine. Sprinkle with the pecorino and serve hot.

■ INGREDIENTS

- 2 tablespoons extra-virgin olive oil
- 200 g (6½ oz) Italian pork sausages, skinned and crumbled
- 1 medium onion, finely chopped
- 2 cloves garlic, finely chopped
- 6 basil leaves, torn
- 500 g (1 lb) peeled and chopped fresh or tinned tomatoes
- salt and freshly ground black pepper
- 4 tablespoons freshly grated pecorino cheese
- 450 g (14 oz) malloreddus

*Wine: a dry red, preferably
Sardinian, such as a Cannonau
(be warned though, Sardinian
wines are notoriously strong.
When aged, they can reach 15-17
percent alcohol content).*

■ INGREDIENTS

- 2 large aubergines (eggplants)
- salt and freshly ground black pepper
- 2 tablespoons extra-virgin olive oil
- 2 cloves garlic, finely chopped
- 400 g (12 oz) peeled and chopped fresh or tinned tomatoes
- 1 tablespoon basil, torn
- vegetable oil for frying
- 50 g (1½ oz) freshly grated pecorino cheese
- 400 g (12 oz) spaghetti

Right:
Malloreddus

Bavette con fagiolini e pesto
Bavette with green beans, potatoes and pesto

If you order pasta with pesto sauce in its hometown of Genoa, it will almost certainly be served with potatoes and green beans.

Serves: 4; Preparation: 15 minutes; Cooking: 25 minutes; Level of difficulty: Simple

Cook the vegetables in a large pot of salted, boiling water until tender. Take them out with a slotted spoon and use the same water to cook the pasta. § While the pasta is cooking, prepare the pesto. Add 2 tablespoons of boiling water from the pasta pot to make the pesto slightly more liquid. § When the pasta is cooked *al dente,* drain and transfer to a heated serving dish. Toss with the pesto, butter and vegetables. Sprinkle with the pecorino and parmesan, and serve hot.

■ INGREDIENTS

• 200 g (6½ oz) green beans, fresh or frozen, cut into short lengths
• 2 medium new potatoes, peeled and diced into small cubes
• 1 quantity of pesto (see recipe p. 28)
• 2 tablespoons butter
• 1 tablespoon freshly grated pecorino cheese
• 1 tablespoon freshly grated parmesan cheese
• 450 g (14 oz) bavette

Wine: a dry white (Vermentino)

Orecchiette con le bietole
Orecchiette with chard

Orecchiette ("little ears") come from Puglia in southern Italy. Like malloreddus, they can also be made at home using bran flour but it is a laborious task. It is much easier to buy them readymade. They are good with the vegetable sauces suggested below, but can also be served with meat sauce (see p. 26), tomato sauces (see p. 22), or garlic, oil and chilli sauce (see p. 38).

Serves: 4; Preparation: 10 minutes; Cooking: 15 minutes; Level of difficulty: Simple

Cook the chard in a pot of salted boiling water (3-4 minutes for frozen, 8-10 minutes for fresh). Drain well and squeeze out any extra moisture. Chop finely. § Combine the garlic and crumbled anchovy fillet in a large sauté pan with the oil. Sauté until the garlic turns gold in colour. Add the chard. Season with salt and pepper. § Cook the orecchiette in a large pot of salted, boiling water until *al dente*. Drain well and transfer to the sauté pan with the sauce. Toss for 1-2 minutes over medium-high heat. Serve immediately with lots of freshly grated pecorino to sprinkle on each portion.

■ INGREDIENTS

• 400 g (12 oz) fresh or 275 g (9 oz) frozen chard (silverbeet)
• 2 cloves garlic, finely chopped
• 6 tablespoons extra-virgin olive oil
• 1 anchovy fillet, crumbled
• salt and freshly ground black pepper
• freshly grated pecorino
• 450 g (14 oz) orecchiette

Wine: dry red (Barolo)

> VARIATIONS
> – If you like hot dishes this one works very well with ½ teaspoon crushed chillies.
> – For slightly different but equally delicious dishes, replace the chard with the same quantity of florets and diced stalks of green broccoli or cauliflower, or shredded savoy cabbage.

Right:
Orecchiette con le bietole

INGREDIENTS

- 500 g (1 lb) asparagus
- 2 tablespoons butter
- 150 g (5 oz) boiled ham, cut into thin strips
- 200 ml (7 fl oz) fresh cream
- 6 tablespoons freshly grated parmesan cheese
- salt and freshly ground black pepper
- 450 g (14 oz) penne

PENNE CON GLI ASPARAGI
Penne with asparagus

Serves: 4; Preparation: 10 minutes; Cooking: 15 minutes; Level of difficulty: Simple

Cook the asparagus in a pot of salted, boiling water until the tips are tender. Drain, and remove the hard parts from each stalk. § Melt the butter in a saucepan with the ham. Cook for 2-3 minutes. Add the asparagus tips and the cream, and stir gently over medium heat for 3-4 minutes, or until the cream thickens. Season with salt and pepper. § Cook the penne in a large pot of salted, boiling water until *al dente*. Drain and place in a heated serving dish. Add the sauce and toss well. Sprinkle with the parmesan and serve hot.

Fusilli lunghi ai porri
Fusilli lunghi with leeks

Serves: 4; Preparation: 10 minutes; Cooking: 40 minutes; Level of difficulty: Simple

Prepare the leeks by discarding two layers of outer leaves and cutting off almost all the top green part. Slice in thin wheels. Set aside. § Combine butter, oil, onion and garlic in a sauté pan and cook over medium heat until the onion turns golden in colour. Add the pancetta and stir so that it browns on all sides. Add the leeks and boiling water (from the pasta pot) and simmer over low heat until the leeks are very tender. Season with salt and pepper. Add the egg yolk and sugar, and stir vigorously. Remove from heat. § Cook the fusilli in a large pot of salted, boiling water until *al dente*. Drain well and transfer to a heated serving dish. Toss with the sauce, sprinkle with pecorino, and serve hot.

Spaghetti alla carrettiera
Spaghetti with onion, garlic and bread crumbs

This is a classic Roman recipe. It is said to have been the favourite dish of the carrettieri *(cart-drivers) who transported the Castelli Romani wine from the Alban Hills into Rome. There are many variations on the basic recipe given here. We have suggested the common tomato one below.*

Serves: 4; Preparation: 10 minutes; Cooking: 15 minutes; Level of difficulty: Simple

Place the onion, garlic and parsley in a sauté pan with the oil, oregano, salt and pepper to taste and sauté over medium heat until the onion and garlic turn golden in colour. Remove from heat. § Toast the bread crumbs in the oven and mix with a few drops of oil. § Cook the spaghetti in a large pot of salted, boiling water until *al dente*. Drain well and transfer to a heated serving dish. Toss with the sauce and bread crumbs, and serve hot.

> VARIATION
> - Add 4 medium peeled tomatoes and ½ teaspoon crushed chillies to the onion and garlic mixture after it has changed colour. Cook over medium heat for 10-15 minutes or until the tomatoes have reduced.

■ INGREDIENTS

- 8 leeks
- 2 tablespoons butter
- 4 tablespoons extra-virgin olive oil
- 1 small onion, finely chopped
- 1 clove garlic, finely chopped
- 100 g (3½ oz) diced pancetta
- 250 ml (8 fl oz) boiling water
- salt and freshly ground black pepper
- 1 egg yolk
- pinch of sugar
- 2 tablespoons freshly grated pecorino cheese
- 450 g (14 oz) fusilli lunghi

Wine: a light, dry red (Lambrusco)

■ INGREDIENTS

- 1 small onion, finely chopped
- 1 clove finely chopped garlic
- 1 tablespoon finely chopped parsley
- 4 tablespoons extra-virgin olive oil
- ½ teaspoon oregano
- salt and freshly ground black pepper
- 2 tablespoons bread crumbs
- 450 g (14 oz) spaghetti

Wine: a dry white (Velletri)

Right:
Fusilli lunghi ai porri

Fresh Pasta

*Fresh pasta is made of egg and soft-wheat flour.
It includes old favourites like tagliatelle, fettuccine
and tagliolini. With a little practice you can
learn to make delicious fresh pasta at home.*

Tagliolini al mascarpone
Tagliolini with mascarpone cheese sauce

The success of this simple sauce lies in the speed and accuracy with which the tagliolini are tossed with the mascarpone and egg. When the pasta comes in contact with the egg, it should still be hot enough to harden the yolk a little so that the whole sauce becomes creamy.

Serves: 4; Preparation: 5 minutes; Cooking: 5 minutes; Level of difficulty: Simple

Warm the mascarpone in a saucepan. Remove from heat and stir in the egg yolk. Season with salt. § Cook the tagliolini in a large pot of salted, boiling water until *al dente*. Drain well and toss with the mascarpone and egg sauce. Sprinkle with the parmesan and freshly ground black pepper. Serve hot.

> VARIATION
> — Add ¼ teaspoon freshly ground nutmeg to the mascarpone and egg.

■ INGREDIENTS

- 120 g (4 oz) fresh mascarpone cheese
- 1 egg yolk
- salt and freshly ground black pepper
- 4 tablespoons freshly grated parmesan cheese
- 450 g (14 oz) shop-bought tagliolini

Wine: a light, dry white (Verdicchio di Matelica)

Tagliatelle alle vongole con panna
Tagliatelle with clams and cream

Serves: 4; Preparation: 10 minutes + time needed to make the pasta; Cooking: 15 minutes; Level of difficulty: Simple

Put the clams in a large sauté pan, cover, and place over high heat until they are all open. Remove from the pan and set aside with their juice. § Sauté the garlic in the same pan over medium heat with the oil, chillies and bay leaves. When the garlic begins to change colour, add the clams and their juice, the cream, tomatoes and salt to taste. Simmer over medium heat for 5-10 minutes, or until the sauce has reduced sufficiently. § Cook the tagliatelle in a large pot of salted, boiling water until *al dente*. Drain well and transfer to the sauté pan with the clams. Toss quickly over medium-high heat and serve immediately.

■ INGREDIENTS

- 1 kg (2 lb) clams
- 1 clove garlic, finely chopped
- 2 tablespoons extra-virgin olive oil
- ½ teaspoon crushed chillies
- 2 bay leaves
- 125 ml (4fl oz) fresh cream
- 2 large tomatoes, peeled and chopped
- salt
- 450 g (14 oz) shop-bought or homemade tagliatelle (see recipe pp. 120-122)

Wine: a dry white (Pinot bianco)

Right:
Tagliolini al mascarpone

Pappardelle sulla lepre
Pappardelle with wild hare sauce

*This is a classic Tuscan dish. Traditionally the recipe calls
for wild hare, but if this is hard to find
use the same amount of rabbit in its place.*

*Serves: 4; Preparation: 20 minutes + time needed to make the pasta; Cooking: 2½ hours; Level of
difficulty: Medium*

Sauté the parsley, rosemary, onion, carrot and celery with the oil in a
heavy-bottomed pan over medium heat. When the onion and garlic
begin to change colour, add the hare meat and cook for 15-20 minutes
or until the meat is well browned, stirring frequently. Add the wine
and stir until it has evaporated. § Add the boiling water, milk and
tomato paste. Season with salt and pepper. Simmer over low heat for
about 1½ hours. § Add the hare liver and, if necessary, more water.
Cook for 30 more minutes or until the hare is very tender. § Cook the
pappardelle in a large pot of salted, boiling water until *al dente*. Drain
well and place in a heated serving dish. Toss with the sauce and
sprinkle with parmesan. Serve hot.

■ INGREDIENTS

• 2 tablespoons parsley, 1
  tablespoon fresh rosemary,
  1 medium onion, 1 small
  carrot, 1 stalk celery, all
  finely chopped
• 6 tablespoons extra-virgin
  olive oil
• 450 g (14 oz) boneless
  wild hare meat, with
  liver, coarsely chopped
• 500 ml (16fl oz) red wine
• 750 ml (24fl oz) boiling
  water
• 60 ml (2fl oz) milk
• 1 tablespoon tomato paste
• salt and freshly ground
  black pepper
• 2 tablespoons freshly
  grated parmesan cheese
• 450 g (14 oz) shop-bought
  or homemade pappardelle
  (see recipe pp. 120-122)

Wine: a dry red (Chianti)

Tagliatelle al prosciutto
Tagliatelle with prosciutto

*Serves: 4; Preparation: 5 minutes + time needed to make the pasta; Cooking: 10-12 minutes; Level
of difficulty: Simple*

Sauté the onion and fat from the prosciutto with the butter in a sauté pan
until the onion begins to change colour. Add the prosciutto and sauté for
2-3 minutes. Add the wine and salt and pepper to taste. Simmer until the
wine evaporates. § Cook the tagliatelle in a large pot of salted boiling water
until *al dente*. Drain well and place in a heated serving dish. Pour the sauce
over the top and toss vigorously. Sprinkle with parmesan and serve hot.

■ INGREDIENTS

• 1 small onion, finely
  chopped
• 150 g (5 oz) diced
  prosciutto
• 50 g (1½ oz) butter
• 125 ml (4fl oz) white wine
• salt and freshly ground
  black pepper
• 2 tablespoons freshly
  grated parmesan cheese
• 450 g (14 oz) shop-bought
  or homemade tagliatelle
  (see recipe pp. 120-122)

*Wine: a rosé
(Rosato di Carmignano)*

*Right:
Pappardelle sulla lepre*

- 100 g (3½ oz) diced pancetta
- 50 g (1½ oz) butter
- 1 clove garlic, finely chopped
- salt and freshly ground black pepper
- 4 tablespoons freshly grated parmesan cheese
- 450 g (14 oz) shop-bought or homemade tagliatelle (see recipe pp. 120-122)

Tagliatelle alla pancetta
Tagliatelle with crispy fried pancetta

Serves: 4; Preparation: 5 minutes + time needed to make the pasta; Cooking: 10-12 minutes; Level of difficulty: Simple

Sauté the pancetta, butter and garlic over medium-high heat in a large sauté pan until the pancetta is crisp. § Cook the tagliatelle in a large pot of salted boiling water until *al dente*. Drain well and transfer to the sauté pan with the pancetta. Toss quickly over medium heat. Sprinkle with the parmesan and season with pepper. Serve hot.

PAGLIA E FIENO SEMPLICE
Paglia e fieno with cream and truffles

Two types of fettuccine, the plain yellow egg variety, and the green spinach variety, are often served together. This colourful mixture is called paglia e fieno, *which means "straw and hay."*

Serves: 4; Preparation: 5 minutes; Cooking: 10 minutes; Level of difficulty: Simple

Melt the butter in a heavy-bottomed pan and add shavings of white truffle. Leave to cook for 1 minute over low heat, then add the cream. Season with salt and pepper. Simmer for 4-5 minutes or until the cream reduces. § Cook the paglia e fieno in a large pot of salted, boiling water until *al dente*. Drain well and add to the pan with the truffle sauce. Sprinkle with the parmesan and toss well over medium heat for 1-2 minutes. Serve hot.

■ INGREDIENTS

- 50 g (1½ oz) butter
- 1 medium white truffle
- 125 ml (4fl oz) fresh cream
- salt and freshly ground black pepper
- 3 tablespoons freshly grated parmesan cheese
- 450 g (14 oz) shop-bought paglia e fieno

Wine: a dry white (Pinot bianco)

PAGLIA E FIENO ALLA TOSCANA
Tuscan-style paglia e fieno

Serves: 4-6; Preparation: 30 minutes; Cooking: 45-50 minutes; Level of difficulty: Medium

Place the pancetta, prosciutto, onion, celery and carrot in a sauté pan with half the butter and cook over medium heat until the onion is transparent. § Add the tomatoes, mushrooms, nutmeg and salt and pepper to taste. Simmer over medium heat for 15 minutes. § Add the wine and, when it has all evaporated, the peas. Cook over medium-low heat until the peas and mushrooms are quite tender, stirring in the meat broth as needed to keep the sauce liquid enough. § Cook the paglia e fieno together in a large pot of salted, boiling water until *al dente*. Drain well and transfer to a heated serving dish. Toss vigorously with the remaining butter. § Place the pasta, sauce and parmesan separately on the table so that everyone can help themselves to as much cheese and sauce as they like.

■ INGREDIENTS

- 50 g (1½ oz) diced pancetta
- 50 g (1½ oz) diced prosciutto
- 1 medium onion, 1 stalk celery, 1 medium carrot, all finely chopped
- 50 g (1½ oz) butter
- 400 g (12 oz) peeled and chopped fresh or canned tomatoes
- 250 g (8 oz) coarsely chopped mushrooms
- pinch of nutmeg
- salt and freshly ground black pepper
- 125 ml (4fl oz) white wine
- 300 g (9½ oz) green peas
- 125 ml (4fl oz) meat broth (see recipe p. 34)
- 5 tablespoons freshly grated parmesan cheese
- 500 g (1 lb) shop-bought paglia e fieno

Right:
Paglia e fieno alla toscana

■ INGREDIENTS

- ½ quantity béchamel sauce (see recipe p. 24)
- 125 ml (4 fl oz) double cream
- 1 tablespoon fresh curry powder
- salt and freshly ground black pepper
- 1 tablespoon butter
- 4 tablespoons freshly grated parmesan cheese
- 450 g (14 oz) shop-bought tagliolini

TAGLIOLINI AL CURRY
Tagliolini with curry sauce

Serves: 4; Preparation: 5 minutes; Cooking: 10 minutes; Level of difficulty: Simple

Prepare the béchamel sauce. Stir the cream and curry powder into the béchamel and cook for 2-3 more minutes. Season with salt and pepper. § Cook the tagliolini in a large pot of salted, boiling water until *al dente*. Drain well and transfer to a heated serving dish. Toss with the butter and the curry sauce. Sprinkle with parmesan and serve immediately.

Tagliatelle verdi primaverili
Spinach tagliatelle with fresh cream, peas and gorgonzola cheese

INGREDIENTS

- 100 g (6½ oz) fresh or frozen peas
- 50 g (1½ oz) gorgonzola cheese
- 250 ml (8fl oz) fresh cream
- salt and freshly ground black pepper
- 1 tablespoon finely chopped parsley
- 5 tablespoons freshly grated parmesan cheese
- 450 g (14 oz) shop-bought or homemade spinach tagliatelle (see recipe pp. 120-122)

Wine: a light, dry white (Soave)

Serves: 4; Preparation: 10 minutes + time needed to make the pasta; Cooking: 15 minutes; Level of difficulty: Simple

Cook the peas in a pot of salted, boiling water. Drain well and set aside. § Place the gorgonzola, diced into 1 cm (½ in) squares, in a large heavy-bottomed pan over low heat. Stir the cheese until it melts. Stir in the cream. Add the peas and salt and pepper to taste. § Cook the pasta in a large pot of salted, boiling water until *al dente*. Drain well and transfer to the pan containing the sauce. Add the parsley and parmesan. Toss well and serve hot.

Maltagliati al ragù di agnello
Maltagliati with lamb sauce

INGREDIENTS

- 3 cloves garlic, finely chopped
- 4 tablespoons extra-virgin olive oil
- 300 g (9½ oz) minced lamb
- 100 g (3½ oz) minced pork
- 1 bay leaf
- 500 g (1 lb) peeled and chopped fresh or tinned tomatoes
- 6 fresh basil leaves
- ½ teaspoon dried marjoram
- salt and freshly ground black pepper
- freshly grated pecorino cheese
- 450 g (14 oz) shop-bought or homemade maltagliati (see recipe pp. 120-122)

Wine: a dry red (Rosso di Montalcino)

Maltagliati (literally "badly cut") are usually served in broth, with minestrone, or pasta soups, but they are sometimes prepared with sauces. In some Italian dialects this pasta is known as spruzzamusi, *or* bagnanasi, *words which are difficult to translate but which mean that you are likely to get broth or sauce on your nose, cheeks and chin.*

Serves: 4; Preparation: 15 minutes + time needed to make the pasta; Cooking: 1¼ hours; Level of difficulty: Simple

Sauté the garlic with the oil in a heavy-bottomed pan over a medium heat until the garlic turns light gold in colour. Add the lamb, pork and bay leaf, and sauté for 8-10 minutes. § Add the tomatoes, basil and marjoram. Season with salt and pepper, and simmer over low heat for an hour. § Cook the maltagliati in a large pot of salted, boiling water until *al dente*. Drain, transfer to a heated serving dish, and toss with the sauce. Serve hot, with lots of pecorino for sprinkling over each portion.

Left: *Tagliatelle verdi primaverili*

TAGLIATELLE ALLA FRANTOIANA
Tagliatelle with olives and mushrooms

Serves: 4; Preparation: 10 minutes + time needed to make the pasta; Cooking: 25 minutes; Level of difficulty: Simple

Combine the garlic and parsley in a sauté pan with the oil and cook over medium-high heat until the garlic begins to change colour. Add the mushrooms and cook until the water they produce has evaporated. § Add the olives, mint, salt and pepper to taste and boiling water. Simmer for 5 minutes. § Cook the tagliatelle in a large pot of salted, boiling water until *al dente*. Drain and transfer to a heated serving dish. Toss vigorously with the sauce and serve at once.

FETTUCCINE ALLA ROMAGNOLA
Fettuccine with simple butter and tomato sauce

The delicate taste of the fettuccine is set off by the butter-based sauce. The simplicity of the dish calls for fine homemade fettuccine. Spinach fettuccine is also good with this sauce.

Serves: 4; Preparation: 5 minutes + time needed to make the pasta; Cooking: 35 minutes; Level of difficulty: Simple

Sauté the garlic and parsley with the butter in a sauté pan. When the garlic begins to change colour, add the tomatoes and season with salt and pepper. Simmer over medium-low heat for about 30 minutes. § Cook the fettuccine in a large pot of salted, boiling water until *al dente*. Drain well and transfer to a heated serving dish. Toss vigorously with the tomato sauce and basil. Serve hot.

VARIATION
– If you are not worried about cholesterol, add a large knob of fresh butter or 2 tablespoons fresh cream to the pasta just before tossing.

■ INGREDIENTS

- 1 clove garlic, finely chopped
- 2 tablespoons finely chopped parsley
- 6 tablespoons extra-virgin olive oil
- 200 g (6½ oz) coarsely chopped mushrooms
- 100 g (3½ oz) pitted and coarsely chopped black olives
- 6 fresh mint leaves, torn
- salt and freshly ground black pepper
- 4 tablespoons boiling water
- 450 g (14 oz) shop-bought or homemade tagliatelle (see recipe pp. 120-122)

Wine: a dry, sparkling red (Lambrusco di Sorbara)

■ INGREDIENTS

- 2 cloves garlic, finely chopped
- 2 tablespoons finely chopped parsley
- 75 g (2½ oz) butter
- 600 g (1¼ lb) peeled and chopped ripe tomatoes
- salt and freshly ground black pepper
- 5 fresh basil leaves, torn
- 450 g (14 oz) homemade fettuccine (see recipe pp. 120-122)

Wine: a young rosé (Castel del Monte)

Right:
Fettuccine alla romagnola

Tagliatelle al sugo d'anatra
Tagliatelle with duck sauce

Serves: 4; Preparation: 20 minutes + time needed to make the pasta; Cooking: 2½ hours; Level of difficulty: Medium

Wash the duck and pat it dry with paper towels. Sprinkle with the oil, salt, pepper, rosemary, sage and bay leaf, and roast in a preheated oven for about an hour. Turn the duck and baste it with the white wine while it is cooking. Remove from the oven and set aside. § Sauté the garlic, onion, carrot and celery in the gravy from the roast duck until the onion is transparent. Add the tomato paste dissolved in a cup of water. Season with salt and pepper. Simmer over medium-low heat for 15 minutes. § Bone the duck and chop the meat coarsely. Add to the pan with the vegetables and cook for 45 more minutes, adding water if necessary. § Cook the tagliatelle in a large pot of salted, boiling water until *al dente*. Drain well and transfer to a heated serving bowl. Pour the sauce over the top and sprinkle with the pecorino. Toss well, and serve hot.

Tagliatelle della duchessa
Tagliatelle with chicken-liver sauce

This recipe comes from Emilia-Romagna in central Italy. It was named after a noblewoman Maria Luigia, Duchess of Parma, who was apparently very fond of it.

Serves: 4; Preparation: 1¼ hours + time needed to make the pasta; Cooking: 15 minutes; Level of difficulty: Medium

Soak the chicken livers for 1 hour in a large bowl of cold water. § Chop the livers finely. Place in a sauté pan with the butter and cook over medium-low heat for 8-10 minutes. Season with salt and pepper. § Cook the tagliatelle in a large pot of salted, boiling water until *al dente*. Drain well and transfer to a heated serving dish. § Add the chicken livers, parmesan and egg yolks. Toss well. The egg yolks shouldn't cook but form a soft creamy sauce. Serve hot.

■ INGREDIENTS

- 1 duck, cleaned and gutted, weighing about 1 kg (2 lb) pounds
- 3 tablespoons extra-virgin olive oil
- salt and freshly ground black pepper
- sprigs of fresh rosemary and sage
- 1 bay leaf
- 250 ml (8fl oz) white wine
- 2 cloves garlic, 1 medium onion, 1 carrot, 1 stalk celery, all finely chopped
- 4 tablespoons tomato paste
- 5 tablespoons freshly grated pecorino cheese
- 450 g (14 oz) shop-bought or homemade tagliatelle (see recipe pp. 120-122)

Wine: a dry red (Sangiovese)

■ INGREDIENTS

- 6 chicken livers
- 150 g (5 oz) butter
- 6 tablespoons freshly grated parmesan cheese
- salt and freshly ground black pepper
- 3 egg yolks
- 450 g (14 oz) shop-bought or homemade tagliatelle (see recipe pp. 120-122)

Wine: a dry red (Cabernet)

Right: *Tagliatelle della duchessa*

FETTUCCINE ALL'ALFREDO
Fettuccine with butter and cream sauce

■ INGREDIENTS

- 50 g (1½ oz) butter
- 250 ml (8fl oz) double cream
- 6 tablespoons freshly grated parmesan cheese
- pinch of nutmeg
- salt and freshly ground black pepper
- 450 g (14 oz) shop-bought or homemade tagliatelle (see recipe pp. 120-122)

Serves: 4; Preparation: 5 minutes + time needed to make the pasta; Cooking: 10 minutes; Level of difficulty: Simple

Place the butter and cream in a heavy-bottomed pan and cook over high heat for 2 minutes. Remove from heat. § Cook the fettuccine in a large pot of salted, boiling water until *al dente*. Drain well and transfer to the pan with the cream. Add the parmesan, nutmeg, salt and pepper to taste, and place over medium-low heat for 1 minute, tossing the pasta constantly. Serve immediately.

Filled Pasta

Filled pasta is made by wrapping small quantities
of meat or vegetable stuffing in delicious fresh, egg pasta.
The various types of ravioli, tortellini and tortelli are
usually served with classic ragù, or simple cream, butter
and herb sauces that won't camouflage the delicate taste
of the pasta and filling.

AGNOLOTTI IN BRODO
Agnolotti in meat broth

Agnolotti are a specialty of the Piedmont region in northern Italy. They are square in shape, like tortelli. They are usually stuffed with meat-based fillings and can be served in meat broth or meat sauces as shown here. They are also good with simple butter and sage sauce (see recipe p. 24), or butter and parmesan sauce (see recipe p. 24).

Serves: 4-6; Preparation: 30 minutes + time needed to make the pasta; Cooking: 15 minutes + 3 hours for the broth; Level of difficulty: Medium

Make the pasta dough. § Combine the onion, celery, carrot and garlic with the butter in a heavy-bottomed pan and sauté over medium heat. When the onion turns light gold, add the pork, veal, liver and bay leaf. Sauté for a few minutes, then add the wine. Cover and simmer over low heat for about 10 minutes, or until the meat is cooked. Remove the meat from the pan. § Put the cooked meat in a blender or food processor and chop finely. Transfer to a mixing bowl. § When cool, add the egg, parmesan and nutmeg and season with salt and pepper. § Prepare the agnolotti as shown on p. 123. § Place the agnolotti in a large pot of boiling meat broth and cook until the pasta around the sealed edges is *al dente*. Transfer the agnolotti and meat broth to a large heated soup dish and serve hot.

■ INGREDIENTS

PASTA: see recipe pp. 120-123
FILLING
• 1 small onion, 1 stalk celery, 1 small carrot, 1 clove garlic, all finely chopped
• 50 g (1½ oz) butter
• 150 g (5 oz) lean pork, 150 g (5 oz) lean veal, 100 g (3½ oz) liver, coarsely chopped
• 1 bay leaf
• 250 ml (8fl oz) dry red wine
• 1 large egg
• 2 tablespoons freshly grated parmesan cheese
• pinch of nutmeg
• salt and freshly ground black pepper
MEAT BROTH: see recipe p. 34

Wine: a dry red (Grignolino)

AGNOLOTTI CON SUGO DI CARNE
Agnolotti with meat sauce

Serves: 4-6; Preparation: 30 minutes + time needed to make the pasta; Cooking: 15 minutes + time needed to make the meat sauce; Level of difficulty: Medium

Make the pasta dough. § Prepare the agnolotti filling as shown above. § Prepare the agnolotti as shown on p. 123. § Prepare the meat sauce. § Cook the agnolotti in a large pot of salted, boiling water until the pasta round the sealed edges is *al dente*. Remove from the water using a slotted spoon and place on a heated serving dish. Cover with the hot meat sauce. Sprinkle with the parmesan and, if you have them, shavings of white truffle. Serve hot.

■ INGREDIENTS

PASTA: see recipe pp. 120-123
FILLING: see above
MEAT SAUCE: see recipe p. 26
• 4 tablespoons freshly grated parmesan cheese
• white truffle (optional)

Wine: a dry red (Dolcetto)

Right:
Agnolotti in brodo

Ravioli semplici al burro
Ravioli with Italian sausage filling in butter and sage sauce

Serves: 4-6; Preparation: 20 minutes + time needed to make the pasta; Cooking: 10 minutes; Level of difficulty: Medium

Make the pasta dough. § Cook the spinach and chard in a pot of salted, boiling water until tender (3-4 minutes if frozen, 8-10 minutes if fresh). Squeeze out excess moisture and chop finely. § Mix the sausages, ricotta, eggs, parmesan and marjoram with the spinach and chard in a mixing bowl. Combine thoroughly and season with salt. § Prepare the ravioli as shown on p. 123. § Cook in a large pot of salted, boiling water until the sealed edges of the ravioli are *al dente*. Drain and transfer to a heated serving dish. § While the ravioli are cooking, prepare the sauce. Pour over ravioli and sprinkle with extra grated parmesan. Serve hot.

> VARIATION
> – *Ravioli semplici* are also very good with meat sauce (see recipe p. 26) or tomato and butter sauce (see recipe p. 22).

INGREDIENTS

PASTA: see recipe pp. 120-123
FILLING
- 200 g (6½ oz) fresh or 125 g (4 oz) frozen spinach
- 600 g (1¼ lb) fresh or 400 g (12 oz) frozen chard (silverbeet)
- 300 g (9½ oz) Italian pork sausages, skinned and crumbled
- 200 g (6½ oz) fresh ricotta cheese
- 2 eggs
- 3 tablespoons freshly grated parmesan cheese
- ½ teaspoon dried marjoram
- salt
BUTTER AND SAGE SAUCE: see recipe p. 24

Wine: a dry red (Freisa)

Ravioli verdi al pomodoro
Spinach ravioli with ricotta cheese filling in tomato and butter sauce

Serves: 4-6; Preparation: 30 minutes + time needed to make the pasta; Cooking: 10 minutes; Level of difficulty: Medium

Make the spinach pasta dough. § Place the ricotta in a mixing bowl. Add the parsley, basil, eggs, nutmeg and salt to taste. Combine the ingredients thoroughly and set aside. § Prepare the tomato and butter sauce. § Prepare the ravioli as shown on p. 123. § Cook in a large pot of salted, boiling water until the sealed edges of the ravioli are *al dente*. Drain well and transfer to a heated serving dish. Pour the hot tomato sauce over the ravioli and toss gently. Sprinkle with parmesan and serve hot.

INGREDIENTS

PASTA: see recipe pp. 120-123
FILLING
- 250 g (8 oz) ricotta cheese
- 120 g (4 oz) parsley and 150 g (5 oz) fresh basil, finely chopped
- 2 eggs
- ¼ teaspoon nutmeg
- salt
- 4 tablespoons freshly grated parmesan cheese
TOMATO AND BUTTER SAUCE: see recipe p. 22

Right: Ravioli semplici al burro

■ INGREDIENTS

PASTA: see recipe pp. 120-123

FILLING

- 450 g (14 oz) ricotta cheese
- 2 eggs
- ¼ teaspoon nutmeg
- 4 tablespoons freshly grated parmesan cheese
- salt

BUTTER AND SAGE SAUCE:
    see recipe p. 24

Wine: a dry white (Frascati)

RAVIOLI DI RICOTTA AL BURRO E SALVIA
Ravioli with ricotta filling in butter and sage sauce

Serves: 4-6; Preparation: 10 minutes + time needed to make the pasta; Cooking: 10 minutes; Level of difficulty: Medium

Make the pasta dough. § Place the ricotta in a mixing bowl and add eggs, nutmeg, parmesan and salt to taste. Combine thoroughly. § Prepare the ravioli as shown on p. 123. § Cook the ravioli in a large pot of salted, boiling water until the pasta around the sealed edges is *al dente*. Drain well and transfer to a heated serving dish. Cover with the sage sauce and extra grated parmesan. Toss gently and serve hot.

■ INGREDIENTS

PASTA: see recipe pp. 120-123
FILLING

• 50 g (1½ oz) boneless lean
  pork, 50 g (1½ oz) chicken
  breast, coarsely chopped
• ¼ cup butter
• 50 g (1½ oz) prosciutto,
  100 g (3½ oz) mortadella,
  finely chopped
• 2 eggs
• 6 tablespoons freshly
  grated parmesan cheese
• ¼ teaspoon nutmeg
• salt and freshly ground
  black pepper
SAUCE

• 50 g (1½ oz) butter
• 125 ml (4fl oz) fresh cream
• 1 small truffle, white or
  black
• 4 tablespoons freshly
  grated parmesan cheese

Wine: a dry white (Galestro)

TORTELLINI ALLA PANNA
Tortellini with cream sauce

Serves: 4-6; Preparation: 25 minutes + time needed to make the pasta; Cooking: 10 minutes; Level of difficulty: Medium

Make the pasta dough. § Put the pork and chicken in a sauté pan with the butter and cook over medium heat for about 5 minutes, or until tender. Remove from the pan and chop finely in a food processor. § Sauté prosciutto and mortadella in the same pan for 2-3 minutes. § Combine pork, chicken, prosciutto and mortadella in a mixing bowl. Add the eggs, parmesan, nutmeg and salt and pepper to taste, and mix thoroughly. Set aside. § Prepare the tortellini as shown on p. 123. § Cook the tortellini in a large pot of salted, boiling water until the sealed edges of the pasta are *al dente*. § To make the sauce, melt the butter in a large saucepan over low heat. Stir in the cream and cook for 2-3 minutes. § When the tortellini are cooked, drain well and transfer to the pan with the cream. Add the parmesan, shavings of truffle, salt and pepper to taste, and toss gently over medium-low heat for 2-3 minutes. Serve hot.

■ INGREDIENTS

PASTA: see recipe pp. 120-123
FILLING: see recipe above
SAUCE

• 150 g (5 oz) peas
• 300 g (9½ oz) coarsely
  chopped mushrooms
• 1 clove garlic, finely
  chopped
• 2 tablespoons finely
  chopped parsley
• 3 tablespoons extra-virgin
  olive oil
• 400 g (12½ oz) tomatoes
• salt and freshly ground
  black pepper

Wine: a dry red (Sangiovese)

Left: *Tortellini alla panna*
and *Tortellini alla boscaiola*

TORTELLINI ALLA BOSCAIOLA
Tortellini with woodsmen-style sauce

Serves: 4-6; Preparation: 25 minutes + time needed to make the pasta; Cooking: 35 minutes; Level of difficulty: Medium

Make the pasta dough. § Make the tortellini filling and set aside. § Cook the peas in boiling water. Drain and set aside. § Put the mushrooms, garlic and parsley in a large sauté pan with the oil and cook for 5 minutes, or until the water the mushrooms produce has evaporated. Add the tomatoes and simmer for about 20 minutes. Add the cooked peas and salt and pepper to taste. Cook for 3-4 more minutes. § While the sauce is cooking, prepare the tortellini as shown on p. 123. § Cook in a large pot of salted, boiling water until sealed pasta edges are *al dente*. Drain well and transfer to the sauté pan. Toss gently and serve immediately.

TORTELLI DI PATATE AL BURRO E SALVIA
Tortelli with potato filling in butter and sage sauce

Serves: 4-6; Preparation: 40 minutes + time needed to make the pasta; Cooking: 10-15 minutes; Level of difficulty: Medium

Make the pasta dough. § Peel the potatoes and cook them in salted, boiling water. § Put the onion and butter in a large sauté pan and cook until the onion begins to change colour. § Mash the potatoes in a mixing bowl and add the onion, half the parmesan, the eggs, nutmeg and a pinch of pepper. Mix thoroughly and set aside to cool. § Prepare the tortelli as shown on p. 123. § Cook the tortelli in a large pot of salted, boiling water until the sealed edges of the pasta are *al dente*. Drain well and transfer to a heated serving dish. § Make the butter and sage sauce and pour over the tortelli. Sprinkle with parmesan and serve hot.

> VARIATION
> – Potato tortelli are also delicious with meat sauce (see recipe p. 26).

TORTELLI CON LE BIETE
Tortelli with chard filling in butter and parmesan sauce

Serves: 4-6; Preparation: 45 minutes + time needed to make the pasta; Cooking: 10-15 minutes; Level of difficulty: Medium

Make the pasta dough. § Cook the chard in a pot of salted, boiling water until tender (3-4 minutes if frozen, 8-10 minutes if fresh). Drain well and squeeze out any extra moisture. Chop finely and place in a mixing bowl. § Add the ricotta, mascarpone, parmesan, eggs and

---

■ INGREDIENTS

PASTA: see recipe pp. 120-123
FILLING
- 600 g (1¼ lb) potatoes
- 1 medium onion
- 50 g (1½ oz) butter
- 6 tablespoons freshly grated parmesan cheese
- 3 eggs
- ¼ teaspoon nutmeg
- freshly ground black pepper

BUTTER AND SAGE SAUCE: see recipe p. 24

Wine: a light, young dry white (Riesling dell'Oltrepò Pavese)

■ INGREDIENTS

PASTA: see recipe pp. 120-123
FILLING
- 500 g (1 lb) fresh or 350 g (11 oz) frozen chard (silverbeet)
- 200 g (6½ oz) fresh ricotta cheese
- 150 g (5 oz) mascarpone cheese

Right:
Tortelli con le biete

nutmeg. Mix thoroughly and add salt to taste. § Prepare the tortelli as shown on p. 123. § Cook the tortelli in a large pot of salted, boiling water until the sealed edges of the pasta are *al dente*. Drain well and transfer to a heated serving dish. Cover with the sauce, toss gently, and serve immediately.

• 6 tablespoons freshly
   grated parmesan cheese
• 2 eggs
• ¼ teaspoon nutmeg
• salt
Butter and parmesan
   sauce: see recipe p. 24

Wine: a dry red
(Brachetto d'Acqui)

Ravioli alle zucchine
Ravioli with courgette filling in butter and rosemary sauce

Serves: 4-6; Preparation: 30 minutes + time needed to make the pasta; Cooking: 10 minutes; Level of difficulty: Medium

Make the pasta dough. § Cook the courgettes in a pot of salted, boiling water until tender. Drain, transfer to a bowl, and mash finely with a fork. Add the amaretti, ricotta, parmesan and nutmeg. Season with salt. Mix well to form a thick cream. If the filling is too liquid, add dry bread crumbs; if it is too thick add a little milk. § Prepare the ravioli as shown on p. 123. § Cook in a large pot of salted, boiling water until the sealed edges of the pasta are *al dente*. Drain well and transfer to a heated serving dish. § While the pasta is cooking, prepare the sauce. Place the garlic in a small saucepan with the butter and rosemary and cook for 3-4 minutes over medium heat, stirring frequently. § Pour the sauce over the ravioli, sprinkle with the parmesan, and serve immediately.

■ INGREDIENTS

PASTA: see recipe pp. 120-123
FILLING
- 2 medium courgettes (zucchini)
- 75 g (2½ oz) crushed amaretti biscuits
- 150 g (5 oz) ricotta cheese
- 75 g (2½ oz) freshly grated parmesan cheese
- ¼ teaspoon nutmeg
- salt
- 4 tablespoons freshly grated parmesan cheese

SAUCE
- 1 clove garlic, finely chopped
- 100 g (3½ oz) butter
- 2 tablespoons finely chopped rosemary

Wine: a dry white (Pinot Bianco)

Agnolini con ripieno di pollo al brodo
Agnolini with chicken filling in chicken broth

Agnolini are also known as agnoli, cappelletti *and* marubini. *The name used in Emilia-Romagna,* cappelletti *("little hats") comes closest to describing their shape. These chicken-filled agnolini served with chicken broth are light and easy to digest.*

Serves: 4-6; Preparation: 35 minutes + time needed to make the pasta; Cooking: 10 minutes + 3 hours for the broth; Level of difficulty: Medium

Make the pasta dough. § Boil the chicken breasts in chicken or meat broth until tender. § Chop finely using a knife or in a food processor. Transfer to a mixing bowl and add eggs, parmesan, nutmeg and salt to taste. Mix thoroughly. § Prepare the agnolini as shown on p. 123. § Cook in a large pot of boiling chicken broth until the sealed edges of the pasta are *al dente*. Transfer to a heated serving dish with the broth and serve hot.

VARIATION
– Also good with butter and parmesan sauce (see recipe p. 24), tomato and butter sauce (see recipe p. 22), and meat sauce (see recipe p. 26).

■ INGREDIENTS

PASTA: see recipe pp. 120-123
FILLING
- 2 boneless, skinless chicken breasts
- 3 eggs
- 90 g (3 oz) freshly grated parmesan cheese
- ¼ teaspoon nutmeg
- salt

BROTH: see recipe p. 34

Wine: a light, dry red (Lambrusco)

Right: *Agnolini con ripieno di pollo al brodo*

RAVIOLI DI PESCE CON SALSA DI VERDURE
Ravioli with fish filling in vegetable sauce

Serves: 4-6; Preparation: 1 hour + time needed to make the pasta; Cooking: 15 minutes; Level of difficulty: Complicated

Make the pasta dough. § Melt the butter in a sauté pan. Add the fish fillets and cook over medium heat for 5 minutes, or until tender. Chop the cooked fish very finely with a knife or in a food processor. § Cook the spinach in a pot of salted water until tender (3-4 minutes if frozen, 8-10 minutes if fresh). Squeeze out excess moisture and chop finely. § Combine the fish and spinach in a bowl with the ricotta, eggs, parmesan and nutmeg. Add salt to taste and mix well. § Prepare the ravioli as shown on p. 123. Set aside. § Put the mushrooms in a small bowl of warm water and leave for 10 minutes. Remove from the water and chop finely. Combine the vegetables with the butter in the sauté pan used to cook the fish, add the tomatoes and a cup of water, and cook over medium-low heat for 20 minutes. Add salt to taste. § Roast the pine nuts in the oven with the flour, and chop finely in a food processor. Add to the tomato sauce. § Cook the ravioli in a large pot of salted, boiling water until the sealed edges of the pasta are *al dente*. Drain well and transfer to a heated serving dish. Pour the sauce over the top, sprinkle with parmesan, and serve immediately.

■ INGREDIENTS

PASTA: see recipe pp. 120-123
FILLING
• 50 g (1½ oz) butter
• 400 g (13 oz) bass fillets
• 300 g (9½ oz) fresh or 200 g (6½ oz) frozen spinach
• 50 g (1½ oz) ricotta cheese
• 2 eggs
• 6 tablespoons freshly grated parmesan cheese
• ¼ teaspoon nutmeg
• salt
SAUCE
• 30 g (1 oz) dried mushrooms
• 1 stalk celery, 1 small onion, 1 tablespoon parsley, all finely chopped
• 100 g (3½ oz) butter
• 2 ripe tomatoes, peeled and chopped
• salt
• 2 tablespoons pine nuts
• ½ tablespoon plain flour
• 5 tablespoons freshly grated parmesan cheese

Wine: a dry white (Cinque Terre)

TORTELLONI VALDOSTANI
Tortelloni with veal, spinach and rosemary filling in cheese sauce

Tortelloni are the same shape as tortellini only larger.
This dish comes from the Val d'Aosta, near the French border in northern Italy.

Serves: 4-6; Preparation: 1½ hours + time needed to make the pasta; Cooking: 5-8 minutes; Level of difficulty: Medium

Make the pasta dough. § Place the rosemary in a sauté pan with the butter and sauté for 2-3 minutes. Add the veal and white wine, and simmer over medium-low heat. When the veal is tender, remove from the

■ INGREDIENTS

PASTA: see recipe pp. 120-123
FILLING
• 1 tablespoon finely chopped fresh rosemary
• 50 g (1½ oz) butter
• 300 g (9½ oz) lean veal
• 2 tablespoons dry white wine
• 250 g (8 oz) fresh or 175 g (5½ oz) frozen spinach
• 1 egg and 1 egg yolk

- 4 tablespoons freshly
  grated parmesan cheese
- dash of nutmeg
- salt and freshly ground
  black pepper

SAUCE

- 100 g (3½ oz) fontina
  cheese
- 50 g (1½ oz) butter
- ¼ teaspoon nutmeg

Above: *Tortelloni valdostani*

pan and chop finely with a knife or in a food processor. § Cook the spinach in a pot of salted water until tender (3-4 minutes if frozen, 8-10 minutes if fresh). Squeeze out excess moisture and chop finely. § Combine the veal and spinach in a bowl and add the eggs, parmesan and nutmeg. Season with salt and pepper. Mix well with a fork and set aside for 1 hour. § Prepare the tortelloni as shown on p. 123. § Cook the tortelloni in a large pot of salted, boiling water until the sealed edges of the pasta are *al dente*. Drain well and transfer to a heated serving dish. § While the pasta is cooking, prepare the sauce. Combine the cheese, butter and nutmeg in a small saucepan over very low heat until the cheese is melted. Pour over the tortelloni and serve hot.

Baked Pasta

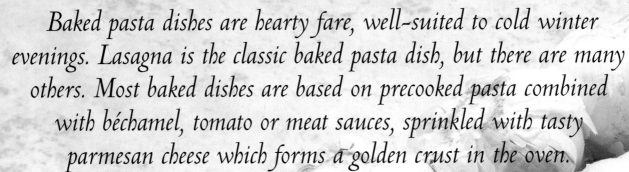

Baked pasta dishes are hearty fare, well-suited to cold winter evenings. Lasagna is the classic baked pasta dish, but there are many others. Most baked dishes are based on precooked pasta combined with béchamel, tomato or meat sauces, sprinkled with tasty parmesan cheese which forms a golden crust in the oven.

Lasagne al forno
Lasagne with Bolognese meat sauce

Serves: 4-6; Preparation: 30 minutes + time needed to make the pasta and the sauce; Cooking: 20 minutes; Level of difficulty: Complicated

Prepare the meat sauce. § Make the pasta dough and prepare the lasagne. § Prepare a large pot of salted, boiling water. Cook the lasagne 4-5 sheets at a time for about 1½ minutes. Remove with a slotted spoon, plunge into a bowl of cold water to stop the cooking process. Remove quickly, and rinse gently under cold running water. Lay the sheets out separately on dry tea towels and pat dry. § Prepare the béchamel and combine with the meat sauce. § Smear the bottom of a large oblong baking dish with butter to prevent the lasagne from sticking. Line with a single layer of cooked lasagne sheets. Cover with a thin layer of meat and béchamel sauce. Sprinkle with grated parmesan, then add another layer of lasagne. Repeat until you have at least 6 layers. Leave enough sauce to spread a thin layer on top. Sprinkle with parmesan and add knobs of butter here and there. § Bake in a preheated oven at 200° C/400° F for 15-20 minutes. A crust should form on the top. Serve hot.

> VARIATIONS
> – For *Lasagne with mushroom sauce* follow the instructions above, replacing the meat sauce with mushroom sauce (see recipe p. 30).
> – For *Lasagne with Genoese basil sauce* follow the instructions above, replacing the meat sauce with basil sauce (see recipe p. 28).

■ INGREDIENTS

MEAT SAUCE: see recipe p. 26

PASTA: 500 g (1 lb) shop-bought dried lasagne sheets or 1 quantity homemade lasagne. See recipe p. 120

- butter to grease the baking dish and for the crust
- 125 g (4 oz) freshly grated parmesan cheese

BÉCHAMEL: see recipe p. 24

Wine: a dry red (Sangiovese)

Rigatoni giganti farciti
Rigatoni giganti filled with meat sauce

You will need a piping bag or syringe to get the filling into the rigatoni.

Serves: 4; Preparation: 35 minutes + time needed to make the sauce; Cooking: 15 minutes; Level of difficulty: Medium

Prepare the meat sauce. § Cook the rigatoni in a large pot of salted, boiling water for half the cooking time indicated on the package. Drain well and place on dry tea towels. § Place the mushrooms and half the butter in a sauté pan and cook over medium-low heat for about 10 minutes, or until

■ INGREDIENTS

- ½ quantity meat sauce (see recipe p. 26)
- 100 g (3½ oz) chopped mushrooms
- 50 g (1½ oz) butter
- 300 g (9½ oz) minced lean beef
- 1 egg
- ½ tablespoon plain flour
- 4 tablespoons white wine

Right:
Rigatoni giganti farciti

- 1 tablespoon tomato paste, dissolved in 1 cup hot water
- salt and freshly ground black pepper
- 4 tablespoons freshly grated parmesan cheese
- 400 g (12 oz) rigatoni giganti

Wine: a dry red
(Chianti dei Colli Fiorentini)

the mushrooms are tender. § Combine the mushrooms with the beef, half the meat sauce, the egg, flour and wine in a heavy-bottomed pan. Mix well. Add all but 1 tablespoon of the tomato and water mixture. Season with salt and pepper. Cover, and cook over medium-low heat for about 15 minutes, stirring frequently with a wooden spoon. Remove from heat. § Fill the piping bag with the mixture and stuff the rigatoni one by one. § Grease an ovenproof dish with butter and place the filled rigatoni in it. Mix the remaining tomato mixture and meat sauce together and pour over the top. Sprinkle with the grated parmesan and dot with the remaining butter. § Bake in a preheated oven at 180° C/350° F for 15 minutes or until a golden crust has formed on top. Serve hot in the ovenproof dish.

■ INGREDIENTS

- 1 clove garlic, finely chopped
- 1 tablespoon finely chopped parsley
- 6 fresh basil leaves, torn
- 4 tablespoons extra-virgin olive oil
- 400 g (12 oz) tomatoes, peeled and chopped
- ½ teaspoon crushed chillies
- salt and freshly ground black pepper
- 100 g (3½ oz) mozzarella cheese, thinly sliced
- 3 tablespoons freshly grated pecorino cheese
- 450 g (14 oz) fusilli

Fusilli con mozzarella e pomodoro
Fusilli with tomatoes and mozzarella cheese

Serves: 4; Preparation: 30 minutes; Cooking: 30 minutes; Level of difficulty: Simple

Combine the garlic, parsley and basil with the oil in a sauté pan and cook over medium heat until the garlic begins to change colour. Add the tomatoes and chillies. Season with salt and pepper. Stir well and simmer over low heat for about 20 minutes, or until sauce has reduced. § Cook the fusilli in a large pot of salted, boiling water for half the time recommended on the package. Drain thoroughly and combine with the tomato sauce. Transfer the mixture to a greased baking dish and arrange the mozzarella over the top. Sprinkle with the pecorino. § Bake in a preheated oven at 180° C/350° F for about 30 minutes, or until the cheese is lightly browned.

■ INGREDIENTS

SAUCE
- ½ quantity tomato and butter sauce (see recipe p. 22)
- 1 quantity béchamel (see recipe p. 24)

FILLING
- 500 g (1 lb) fresh or 350 g (11 oz) frozen spinach
- 50 g (1½ oz) butter
- 300 g (9½ oz) fresh ricotta cheese
- 90 g (3 oz) freshly grated parmesan cheese
- 2 eggs
- salt and freshly ground black pepper
- 12 shop-bought cannelloni, spinach or plain

Wine: a light, dry red (Vino Novello)

Left:
Cannelloni di ricotta e spinaci

Cannelloni di ricotta e spinaci
Cannelloni with ricotta and spinach filling in tomato and béchamel sauce

Serves: 4-6; Preparation: 40 minutes; Cooking: 20 minutes; Level of difficulty: Medium

Prepare the tomato sauce. § Cook the spinach in a pot of salted water until tender (3-4 minutes if frozen, 8-10 minutes if fresh). Drain, squeeze out excess moisture and chop finely. § Put half the butter in a sauté pan with the spinach. Season with salt and pepper. Cook briefly over high heat until the spinach has absorbed the flavour of the butter. § Transfer to a bowl and mix well with the ricotta, half the parmesan and the eggs. § Prepare the béchamel. § Cook the cannelloni in a large pot of salted, boiling water until half-cooked (about 5 minutes). Drain, and pass the colander with the pasta under cold running water. Dry the cannelloni with paper towels and stuff with the ricotta and spinach. § Line the bottom of an ovenproof dish with a layer of béchamel and place the cannelloni in a single layer on it. Cover with alternate spoonfuls of béchamel and tomato sauce. Sprinkle with the remaining parmesan and dot with butter. § Cook at 200° C/400°F for 20 minutes or until a golden crust has formed on the top. Serve hot.

VARIATION
– Replace tomato sauce with a ½ quantity of meat sauce (see recipe p. 26).

Penne gratinate al forno
Baked penne rigate

Serves: 4; Preparation: 30 minutes; Cooking: 30 minutes; Level of difficulty: Simple

Sauté the parsley, onion and garlic with the oil in a sauté pan until lightly browned. Add the tomatoes and simmer over low heat for 25 minutes. § Cook the penne in a large pot of salted, boiling water for half the time shown on the package. Drain well. § Place a layer of pasta in a greased baking dish. Cover with a layer of pancetta, tomato mixture and both cheeses. Repeat layers until the dish is full, reserving a little of both cheeses to sprinkle on top. They will turn golden brown in the oven. Bake in a preheated oven at 180° C/350° F for 30 minutes and serve piping hot.

■ INGREDIENTS

- 2 tablespoons parsley, 1 small onion, 1 clove garlic, all finely chopped
- 4 tablespoons extra-virgin olive oil
- 500 g (1 lb) peeled and diced tomatoes
- salt and freshly ground black pepper
- 100 g (3½ oz) diced pancetta
- 250 g (8 oz) diced mozzarella cheese
- 60 g (2 oz) freshly grated pecorino cheese
- 450 g (14 oz) penne rigate

Maccheroni incaciati
Maccheroni baked with veal, salame, eggs, mozzarella cheese and vegetables

Serves: 4-6; Preparation: 1½ hours; Cooking 20 minutes; Level of difficulty: Simple

To take away the harsh taste of the aubergines, sprinkle each slice with salt and place in a large bowl. Cover, and set aside for an hour. § Put the slices on a cutting board and peel with a knife. Rinse under cold running water and pat dry with paper towels. § Dust the slices with flour. Heat the vegetable oil in a large sauté pan until very hot and add the aubergine. Sauté until golden brown on both sides. Remove from the pan and place on a platter covered with paper towels. § Grease a deep-sided ovenproof dish with a little oil and line the bottom with slices of fried aubergine. § Cook the garlic in a large sauté pan with the olive oil until it begins to change colour. Add the tomatoes, veal, salame, peas and basil and simmer over medium-low heat for about 30 minutes, stirring occasionally with a wooden spoon. Add the chopped chicken livers and cook for 5 more minutes. § Cook the maccheroni in a large pot of salted, boiling water for half the cooking time indicated on the package. Drain well. § Mix with the sauce, eggs and any remaining aubergine slices. Pour into the baking dish with the aubergine. Cover with the mozzarella and pecorino. Bake in a preheated oven at 200° C/400° F for about 20 minutes, or until a golden crust has formed on top. Serve hot in the baking dish.

■ INGREDIENTS

- 2 medium aubergines (eggplants), cut into ½ cm (¼ in) thick slices
- salt and freshly ground black pepper
- 4 tablespoons plain flour
- vegetable oil for frying
- 1 clove garlic, chopped
- 4 tablespoons extra-virgin olive oil
- 400 g (12 oz) tomatoes
- 100 g (3½ oz) coarsely chopped veal
- 80 g (3 oz) diced salame
- 100 g (3½ oz) peas
- 4 basil leaves, torn
- 100 g (3½ oz) coarsely chopped chicken livers
- 2 boiled eggs, sliced
- 150 g (5 oz) mozzarella cheese, sliced
- 4 tablespoons freshly grated pecorino cheese
- 450 g (14 oz) maccheroni

Right: *Penne gratinate al forno*

Timballo di maccheroni alla ferrarese
Maccheroni with meat sauce, béchamel and truffles baked in pastry casing

■ INGREDIENTS

MEAT SAUCE: see recipe
p. 26

BÉCHAMEL: see recipe p. 24

PASTRY: see recipe for
Timballo di gnocchi
p. 110

• 25 g (1 oz) butter
• 1½ tablespoons
breadcrumbs
• 1 whole white truffle
• 90 g (3 oz) freshly grated
parmesan cheese
• 500 g (1 lb) maccheroni

*Wine: a dry red
(Barbaresco)*

Serves: 4-6; Preparation: 30 minutes + time needed to make sauces; Cooking: 30 minutes; Level of difficulty: Complicated

Prepare a ½ quantity of meat sauce and a ½ quantity of béchamel. § Prepare the pastry dough. § Cook the maccheroni in a large pot of salted, boiling water for half the time indicated on the package. Drain well and mix with half the meat sauce. § Grease an ovenproof baking dish with butter and sprinkle with finely ground breadcrumbs. Roll the dough out to about ⅛ inch thick and line the baking dish. Line the bottom with a layer of béchamel, then cover with pasta and meat sauce. Sprinkle with fine shavings of truffle. Repeat until all the ingredients are in the baking dish. The last layer should be of béchamel. Sprinkle with the parmesan. § Bake in a preheated oven at 180° C/ 350° F for about 30 minutes. Serve hot.

Strudel di spinaci al forno
Baked spinach and ricotta roll

■ INGREDIENTS

PASTA: see recipe pp. 120-121

FILLING
• 800 g (1¾ lb) fresh or 500 g
(1 lb) frozen spinach
• 250 g (8 oz) fresh ricotta
cheese
• 3 tablespoons freshly
grated parmesan cheese
• ¼ teaspoon nutmeg
• salt

Right:
Strudel di spinaci al forno

Serves: 4-6; Preparation: 1 hour; Cooking: 45 minutes; Level of difficulty: Complicated

Make the pasta. § Cook the spinach in a pot of salted water until tender (3-4 minutes if frozen, 8-10 minutes if fresh). Drain, squeeze out excess moisture and chop finely. § Put the spinach in a bowl and add the ricotta, parmesan and nutmeg. Combine thoroughly and season with salt. § Lightly flour a table top or flat work surface and roll the pasta dough out until it is very thin. Cut the dough into a rectangle about 30 x 40 cm (12 x 16 in). § Spread the spinach and ricotta mixture evenly over the top and roll it up. Seal the ends by squeezing the dough

BÉCHAMEL: see recipe p. 24

TOMATO AND BUTTER
  SAUCE: see recipe p. 22

*Wine: a dry red
(Collio Merlot)*

together. Wrap the roll tightly in cheesecloth, tying the ends with string. § Bring a large pot of salted water to a boil. The pot should be wide enough so that the roll can lie flat. Immerse the roll carefully into the boiling water and simmer for about 20 minutes. Remove from the pot and set aside. § While the roll is cooking, prepare half quantities of béchamel and tomato sauces. § Unwrap the spinach roll and cut into slices about 1 cm (½ in) thick. Cover the bottom of an ovenproof dish with a layer of béchamel and top with slices of spinach roll. Mix the remaining béchamel with the tomato sauce and cover the spinach slices. Sprinkle with extra parmesan and bake in a preheated oven at 180° C/350° F for about 15 minutes, or until a golden crust forms on top. Serve hot.

Pasticcio di maltagliati al prosciutto
Baked maltagliati with ham, cream and eggs

■ INGREDIENTS

• 50 g (1½ oz) butter
• 4 eggs, separated
• 200 g (6½ oz) finely chopped boiled ham
• 2 tablespoons finely chopped parsley
• pinch of nutmeg
• salt and freshly ground black pepper
• 250 ml (8fl oz) fresh cream
• 4 tablespoons freshly grated parmesan cheese
• 450 g (14 oz) shop-bought dried maltagliati

Wine: a dry red
(Chianti Classico)

Serves: 4; Preparation: 15 minutes; Cooking: 1 hour; Level of difficulty: Medium

Melt the butter in a saucepan over low heat. Add the egg yolks, ham and parsley, and stir with a wooden spoon for 2-3 minutes. Add the nutmeg and season with salt and pepper. Remove from heat. § Whip the cream until stiff. In a separate bowl, beat the egg whites until stiff. Gently stir the whipped cream into the egg whites and add to the butter mixture. § Cook the pasta in a large pot of salted, boiling water for half the recommended time. Drain well and place on dry tea towels. § Grease an ovenproof dish with butter and place the pasta in it. Cover with the egg, cream and ham mixture. Sprinkle with the parmesan cheese. Bake in a preheated oven at 180° C/350° F for about 50 minutes. Serve in the ovenproof dish.

VARIATION
– Replace the cream and egg whites with 1 quantity of béchamel sauce (see recipe p. 24).

Pomodori ripieni di pasta
Baked tomatoes with pasta filling

■ INGREDIENTS

• 8 medium tomatoes
• 8 basil leaves
• 2 tablespoons finely chopped parsley
• 3 tablespoons extra-virgin olive oil
• salt and freshly ground black pepper
• 8 tablespoons ditaloni rigati or other small, tubular pasta

Wine: a dry white
(Frascati)

Choose firm, red tomatoes with their stalks still attached for this tasty, baked tomato dish. The tomatoes can be served hot straight from the oven or left to cool and served as a cold entrée.

Serves: 4; Preparation: 20 minutes; Cooking: 40 minutes; Level of difficulty: Simple

Rinse the tomatoes and dry well. Cut the top off each tomato (with its stalk) and set aside. Hollow out the insides of the bottom parts with a teaspoon. Put the pulp in a bowl. § Place a basil leaf in the bottom of each hollow shell. § Cook the pasta in a medium pot of salted, boiling water for half the time indicated on the package. Drain well. § Combine the pasta with the tomato mixture. Add the parsley and 2 tablespoons of the oil. Season with salt and pepper. § Stuff the hollow tomatoes with the mixture. § Grease an ovenproof dish with the remaining oil and carefully place the tomatoes on it. Cover with the tomato tops. § Bake for about 40 minutes in a preheated oven at 180° C/350° F. Serve either hot or cold.

Right:
Pomodori ripieni di pasta

GNOCCHI

The most common type of gnocchi are the white potato ones, made with mashed potatoes and flour. But there are also spinach gnocchi, ricotta gnocchi, baked semolina gnocchi and fried gnocchi.

Gnocchi di patate al gorgonzola
Potato gnocchi with gorgonzola cheese sauce

Potato gnocchi are a simple mixture of boiled, mashed potatoes and flour. They are made in the same way throughout Italy, although in some regions eggs are added to the basic dough. The choice of potato is important. Don't use new potatoes or baking potatoes; the humble boiling potato is best. Besides the cheese-based sauces given below, potato gnocchi are also good with tomato and butter sauce (see p. 22), pesto (see p. 28), and meat sauce (see p. 26).

Serves: 6; Preparation: 20 minutes; Cooking: 35 minutes; Level of difficulty: Medium

Cook the potatoes in their skins in a pot of salted, boiling water for 20 minutes, or until tender. Drain and peel while still hot. Mash until smooth. Place on a flat work surface and add most of the flour. Knead the mixture, adding more flour as required, until it is soft and smooth, but just slightly sticky. The amount of flour required will depend on how much the potatoes can absorb, so don't add it all at once. § Dust the work surface with flour, take a piece of the dough and roll it into a long sausage about 2 cm (¾ in) in diameter. Cut into pieces about 2.5 cm (1 in) in length. Repeat until all the dough has been made into gnocchi. § Set a large pot of salted water over high heat to boil. The gnocchi should be cooked in 4 or 5 batches. When the water is boiling, lower the first batch (20-24 gnocchi) gently into the water. After a few minutes they will rise to the top. Leave them to bob about for about a minute or two, then scoop them out with a slotted spoon. Place on a heated serving dish. Repeat until all the gnocchi are cooked. § Put the gorgonzola and butter into a heavy-bottomed pan. Place over low heat and stir gently with a wooden spoon until the cheese and butter have melted. Add the cream and cook over medium low heat for 3-4 minutes, or until the cream has reduced and the sauce is thick and creamy. Season with salt and pepper. § Pour over the gnocchi on the serving dish. Sprinkle with parmesan and serve immediately.

■ INGREDIENTS

Gnocchi
- 800 g (1½ lb) boiling potatoes
- approximately 250 g (8 oz) plain flour

Sauce
- 100 g (3½ oz) gorgonzola cheese
- 50 g (1½ oz) butter
- 150 ml (5fl oz) fresh cream
- salt and freshly ground black pepper
- 6 tablespoons freshly grated parmesan cheese

Wine: a dry white (Corvo di Salaparuta)

VARIATIONS
– For richer gnocchi, add 150 g (5 oz) melted butter and 3 eggs to the basic dough. Prepare as above. You may need a little more flour. This will make *Gnocchi alla piemontese* (Piedmont-style gnocchi).
– Add 20 shelled and chopped walnuts to the gorgonzola and butter before adding the cream.

Right:
Gnocchi di patate al gorgonzola

INGREDIENTS

GNOCCHI: see recipe p. 106

SAUCE

- ½ quantity of béchamel sauce (see recipe p. 24)
- 150 g (5 oz) chopped fontina cheese
- 100 g (3½ oz) chopped gorgonzola cheese
- 100 g (3½ oz) mascarpone cheese
- 8 tablespoons freshly grated parmesan cheese
- salt and black pepper

GNOCCHI DI PATATE AI QUATTRO FORMAGGI
Potato gnocchi with four-cheese sauce

Serves: 6; Preparation: 20 minutes; Cooking: 30 minutes; Level of difficulty: Medium

Prepare the potato gnocchi. § Prepare the béchamel sauce. Add the four cheeses and stir over low heat until they have melted and the sauce is smooth and creamy. Season with salt and pepper. § Cook the gnocchi in a large pot of salted, boiling water following the instructions on the previous page. When all the gnocchi are cooked and laid out on a heated serving dish, pour the cheese sauce over the top and toss gently. Serve hot.

Gnocchi di patate e spinaci al burro e salvia
Potato and spinach gnocchi in butter and sage sauce

Serves: 6; Preparation: 20 minutes; Cooking: 50 minutes; Level of difficulty: Medium

Cook the potatoes in their skins in a pot of salted, boiling water for 20 minutes, or until tender. Drain and peel while hot. § Cook the spinach in a pot of salted water until tender (3-4 minutes if frozen, 8-10 minutes if fresh). Drain and squeeze out excess moisture. § Purée the potatoes and spinach together in a food mill. Place the mixture on a flat work surface. Work the eggs and flour in gradually. Add the nutmeg. Season with salt and pepper. Knead the mixture until smooth. § To prepare and cook the gnocchi, follow the instructions for potato gnocchi on p. 106. § When the gnocchi are cooked, quickly prepare the butter and sage sauce. Pour over the gnocchi and toss gently. Sprinkle with parmesan and serve hot.

■ INGREDIENTS

GNOCCHI
• 500 g (1 lb) boiling potatoes
• 500 g (1 lb) fresh or 350 g (11 oz) frozen spinach
• 2 eggs
• approximately 75 g (2½ oz) plain flour
• 50 g (1½ oz) butter
• pinch of nutmeg
• salt and freshly ground black pepper
• 2 tablespoons freshly grated parmesan cheese

BUTTER AND SAGE SAUCE: see recipe p. 24

Wine: a dry red (Rosso dei vigneti del Brunello)

Gnocchi di spinaci e ricotta al pomodoro
Spinach and ricotta gnocchi in tomato and butter sauce

Serves: 6; Preparation: 45 minutes; Cooking: 25 minutes; Level of difficulty: Medium

Prepare the tomato and butter sauce. § Put the onion in a saucepan with the butter and sauté over medium heat until it turns golden brown. Remove the onion with a fork, leaving as much butter as possible in the pan. § Cook the spinach in a pot of salted water until tender (3-4 minutes if frozen, 8-10 minutes if fresh). Drain and squeeze out excess moisture. Chop finely. § Add the spinach to the pan with the butter. Sauté over medium-low heat for 10 minutes. Remove from heat and set aside. § When the spinach is cool, put it in a bowl with the ricotta, eggs, nutmeg and all but 4 tablespoons of parmesan. Season with salt and pepper and mix well. Stir in the flour gradually until the dough is firm. § Lightly dust your hands with flour and roll pieces of dough into walnut-size balls. If the dough sticks to your hands, put it back into the bowl and add more flour. Place the gnocchi on a lightly floured platter. § Cook the gnocchi following the instructions on p. 106 for potato gnocchi. § Reheat the tomato sauce. Toss gently with the gnocchi. Sprinkle with the remaining parmesan and serve hot.

■ INGREDIENTS

TOMATO AND BUTTER SAUCE : see recipe p. 22

GNOCCHI
• 1 small onion, sliced in thin rings
• 50 g (1½ oz) butter
• 800 g (1¾ lb) fresh or 500 g (1 lb) frozen spinach
• 200 g (6½ oz) fresh ricotta cheese
• 3 eggs
• pinch of nutmeg
• 300 g (9½ oz) freshly grated parmesan cheese
• salt and freshly ground black pepper
• approximately 300 g (9½ oz) plain flour

Wine: a dry red (Lambrusco)

Right:
Gnocchi di patate e spinaci al burro e salvia

TIMBALLO DI GNOCCHI
Potato gnocchi in béchamel sauce baked in a pastry casing

■ INGREDIENTS

GNOCCHI: see Potato
gnocchi p. 106

PASTRY
• 250 g (8 oz) plain flour
• 100 g (3½ oz) butter
• 2 egg yolks
• finely grated rind of 1
  lemon
• salt

BÉCHAMEL: see recipe p. 24

• 4 tablespoons freshly
  grated parmesan cheese
• 50 g (1½ oz) butter

*Wine: a dry red
(Chianti delle Colline Pisane)*

Serves: 6; Preparation: 1 hour; Cooking: 1 hour; Level of difficulty: Complicated

Sift the flour into a mixing bowl with the eggs, lemon rind, and salt. Add the butter and mix well. When the dough is moist and firm but not sticky, roll it into a ball, cover with cling film, and place in the fridge for an hour. § Roll the dough out until it is about 1 cm (½ in) thick. Grease the bottom and sides of a baking dish with butter and line with the dough. Prick well with a fork so that it doesn't swell while in the oven. § Bake in a preheated oven at 200° C/400° F for about 20 minutes, or until the pastry is golden brown. § Prepare and cook the potato gnocchi. § Prepare 1 quantity of béchamel sauce. § Put the cooked gnocchi in the béchamel and mix gently. Transfer to the baking dish with the pastry. Sprinkle with the parmesan cheese. Return to the oven and bake for 10 minutes more. Remove from the oven and slip the pastry casing containing the gnocchi out of the baking dish. Serve hot.

GNOCCHI DI LATTE
Fried gnocchi

■ INGREDIENTS

• 1 egg and 5 egg yolks
• 1 tablespoon sugar
• 100 g (3½ oz) potato
  flour
• 500 ml (16fl oz) milk
• 150 g (5 oz) butter
• ¼ teaspoon nutmeg
• ¼ teaspoon cinnamon
• salt
• 4 tablespoons plain flour
• 6 tablespoons breadrumbs
• 4 tablespoons freshly
  grated parmesan cheese

Wine: a dry red (Collio Merlot)

Right:
*Timballo di gnocchi
and Gnocchi di latte*

Serves: 4-6; Preparation: 50 minutes; Cooking: 40 minutes; Level of difficulty: Medium

Beat 5 egg yolks in a bowl with the sugar until smooth. § Place the potato flour in a heavy-bottomed pan. Stir the milk in gradually. Add the egg mixture, 2 tablespoons of the butter, the nutmeg, cinnamon and salt. Mix well with a wooden spoon. § Place the pan over medium heat and, stirring continually, bring to the boil. Boil for 10 minutes, stirring all the time. Remove from heat. § Turn the gnocchi batter out onto a flat work surface. Using a spatula dipped in cold water, spread it to a thickness of about 1 cm (½ in) and leave to cool for 30 minutes. § Cut the batter into 1 cm (½ in) cubes. Beat the remaining egg in a bowl with a fork. Dust the gnocchi with flour, drop them into the beaten egg, then roll them in breadcrumbs. § Fry the gnocchi in the remaining butter until they are golden brown. Place on a heated serving dish. Sprinkle with parmesan and serve immediately.

GNOCCHI ALLA ROMANA
Baked semolina gnocchi

Serves: 6; Preparation: 25 minutes; Cooking: 45 minutes; Level of difficulty: Medium

Put the milk and 1½ tablespoons of the butter in a heavy-bottomed pan and bring to a boil. Add the semolina very gradually just as the milk is beginning to boil. Stirring continually, cook over low heat for 15-20 minutes, or until the mixture is thick and no longer sticks to the sides of the pan. § Remove from heat and leave to cool for 2-3 minutes. Add the egg yolks, salt, 2 tablespoons of the parmesan and 2 tablespoons of the gruyère and mix well. § Wet a flat work surface with cold water and turn the gnocchi batter out onto it. Using a spatula dipped in cold water, spread it out to a thickness of about 1 cm (½ in). Leave the batter to cool to room temperature. § Use a biscuit cutter or small glass with a diameter of about 4-5 cm (1½-2 in) to cut the gnocchi into round disks. § Grease a baking dish with butter and place a row of gnocchi at one end. Lean the next row of gnocchi on the bottoms of the first, roof-tile fashion. Repeat until the baking dish is full. § Melt the remaining butter and pour over the gnocchi. Sprinkle with the remaining parmesan and gruyère. § Bake in a preheated oven at 200° C/400° F for about 20 minutes, or until a golden crust forms on top. Serve hot.

■ INGREDIENTS

- 1 litre (1¾ pints) milk
- 100 g (3½ oz) butter
- 300 g (9½ oz) semolina
- 4 egg yolks
- 1 teaspoon salt
- 6 tablespoons freshly grated parmesan cheese
- 6 tablespoons freshly grated gruyère cheese

*Wine: a dry red
(Merlot di Aprilia)*

GNOCCHI ALLA BAVA
Baked potato gnocchi

Serves: 6; Preparation: 25 minutes; Cooking: 40 minutes; Level of difficulty: Medium

Prepare and cook the potato gnocchi. Place them in a greased baking dish and cover with the sliced fontina. Dot with butter and sprinkle with the parmesan. § Bake in a preheated oven at 220° C/425° F for about 10 minutes, or until a golden crust has formed. Serve hot.

VARIATIONS
– Melt half the butter with a clove of finely chopped garlic and pour over the gnocchi before adding the cheese.
– Spinach and ricotta gnocchi can also be baked in the same way (see recipe p. 108).

■ INGREDIENTS

POTATO GNOCCHI:
see recipe p. 106

SAUCE
- 150 g (5 oz) fontina cheese, sliced thinly
- 100 g (3½ oz) butter
- 6 tablespoons freshly grated parmesan cheese

*Wine: a dry red
(Barbaresco)*

Right:
Gnocchi alla romana

Soups and Salads

Satisfying and nourishing, hot pasta soups are lighter than most other pasta dishes. They are usually served with parmesan and a dash of oil. Pasta salads make great lunches, barbecue fillers, or starters for evening meals on hot summer nights.

Minestra di pasta e fagioli
Pasta and bean soup

Serves 4; Preparation: 5 minutes; Cooking 25 minutes + overnight soaking & cooking if using dried beans; Level of difficulty: Simple

Purée three-quarters of the beans in a food mill or blender. § Combine the onion and rosemary in a heavy-bottomed pan with the oil and sauté briefly over high heat. Before the onion begins to change colour, add the puréed beans, tomato, and, if necessary, one or two cups of water. Season with salt and pepper and simmer over medium-low heat for about 15 minutes. § Add the pasta and remaining whole beans, and cook for 6-7 minutes, or until the pasta is cooked. Serve hot.

VARIATION
– For a heartier soup, add 50 g (1½ oz) finely chopped pancetta to the onion and rosemary mixture.

Minestrone di verdura
Vegetable soup

This soup is a delicious and healthy appetizer for family dinners on cold winter evenings. Served at lunch with crunchy fresh bread, it is a meal-in-itself. In Tuscany, where the olive oil is particularly tasty, cooks add a dash of oil to each portion.

Serves 6; Preparation: 20 minutes + overnight soaking & cooking if using dried beans; Cooking 1 hour; Level of difficulty: Simple

Combine the celery, parsley, basil, onion, garlic and carrot with the oil in a large, heavy-bottomed saucepan. Sauté for 2-3 minutes over medium heat. Add the cabbage and the carrot wheels. Sauté for another 2-3 minutes. Add the courgettes, peas, green beans, and boiling water. Simmer for 10 minutes. § Add the tomatoes and potatoes. Season with salt and pepper and simmer over medium-low heat for about 35 minutes, or until the vegetables are almost tender. § Add the spinach, kidney beans, and pasta and simmer for 7-8 minutes, or until the pasta is cooked *al dente*. Sprinkle with parmesan and serve hot.

■ INGREDIENTS

- 500 g (1 lb) white or red kidney beans, canned, or soaked and precooked as shown on the next page
- 1 small onion, finely chopped
- 1 tablespoon finely chopped fresh rosemary
- 4 tablespoons extra-virgin olive oil
- 1 ripe tomato, peeled and chopped
- salt and freshly ground black pepper
- 200 g (6½ oz) mezzi rigatoni or other small, tubular pasta

Wine: a dry white (Tocai di Lison)

■ INGREDIENTS

- 1 stalk celery, 1 tablespoon parsley, 4-5 fresh basil leaves, 1 medium onion, 1 clove garlic, 1 medium carrot, all finely chopped
- 4 tablespoons extra-virgin olive oil
- 8 ounces savoy cabbage, chopped in thin strips
- 1 carrot, sliced in wheels
- 2 small courgettes (zucchini), diced
- 200 g (6½ oz) peas
- 150 g (5 oz) sliced green beans
- 2 litres (3½ pints) boiling water

Right:
Minestrone di verdura

- 2 large tomatoes, peeled and chopped
- 2 medium potatoes, diced
- salt and freshly ground black pepper
- 300 g (9½ oz) spinach, torn
- 150 g (5 oz) kidney beans, canned, or soaked and precooked as shown here
- 2 tablespoons freshly grated parmesan cheese
- 200 g (6½ oz) soup pasta

Wine: a young, dry red

Soaking and cooking beans

If you have the time, dried beans soaked overnight and precooked will make both these soups more appetizing than if you use the bland and pulpy canned varieties.

Place the beans in a large bowl with at least 8 cm (3 in) of water over the top. Cover with a tea towel and leave overnight. § Drain and rinse well under cold water. Place in a large pot of cold water, cover, and bring to the boil over medium heat. § Simmer over low heat for about 50 minutes, or until the beans are tender but not mushy. Add salt about 10 minutes before the beans are cooked.

Insalata di ruote con le verdure
Ruote salad with vegetables

Serves 4; Preparation: 15 minutes; Cooking 15 minutes; Level of difficulty: Simple

Cook the ruote in a large pot of salted, boiling water until *al dente*. Drain thoroughly. Transfer to a large salad bowl and toss vigorously with half the oil. Set aside to cool. § Cut the stalk and hard base off the aubergine and peel. Cut crosswise into slices about 1 cm (½ in) thick. Place the slices under the broiler and broil for about 10 minutes, or until tender. Dice the cooked slices in 2 cm (¾ in) squares. § Quarter the bell peppers lengthwise and slice each quarter into thin strips. Slice the white, bottom part of the shallot very finely. § Combine the remaining oil, capers, oregano, parsley, aubergine, peppers and pecorino with the pasta. Sprinkle with salt and pepper. Make sure the salad is completely cool before serving.

■ INGREDIENTS

- 6 tablespoons extra-virgin olive oil
- 1 medium aubergine (eggplant)
- 1 small yellow and 1 small red pepper
- 1 shallot
- 1½ tablespoons capers
- ½ teaspoon dried oregano
- 1 tablespoon finely chopped parsley
- 2 tablespoons freshly grated pecorino cheese
- salt and freshly ground black pepper
- 450 g (14 oz) ruote, plain, wholewheat or coloured

Wine: a dry, young white (Frascati)

Insalata di fusilli con pomodori, aglio e mozzarella
Fusilli salad with tomato, garlic and mozzarella cheese

Serves 4; Preparation: 10 minutes; Cooking 10 minutes; Level of difficulty: Simple

Cook the fusilli in a large pot of salted, boiling water until *al dente*. Drain well. Transfer to a large salad bowl and toss vigorously with half the oil. Set aside to cool. § Cut the tomatoes into bite-size pieces and add to the pasta. Combine the garlic and parsley with the remainder of the oil and a sprinkling of salt, and add to the salad bowl. Leave to cool completely. § Just before serving, dice the mozzarella into 1 cm (½ in) cubes on a cutting board. Slant the board slightly so that the extra liquid runs off. Sprinkle over the top of the salad with the torn basil leaves and freshly ground black pepper. Serve cool.

■ INGREDIENTS

- salt and freshly ground black pepper
- 4 tablespoons extra-virgin olive oil
- 2 large ripe tomatoes
- 1 clove garlic, finely chopped
- 1 tablespoon finely chopped parsley
- 250 g (8 oz) mozzarella cheese
- 5 fresh basil leaves
- 450 g (14 oz) fusilli, plain, wholewheat or coloured

VARIATION
– Add 1 tablespoon mustard to the oil for a sharper flavour.

Right:
Insalata di ruote con le verdure
and *Insalata di fusilli con pomodori*

■ INGREDIENTS

- salt
- 2 tablespoons extra-virgin olive oil
- 3 boiled eggs
- 2 large ripe tomatoes
- 150 g (5 oz) tuna, preserved in oil
- 1 shallot
- 3 tablespoons mayonnaise
- 1 tablespoon finely chopped parsley
- 450 g (14 oz) conchiglie

Insalata di conchiglie splendida

Conchiglie with eggs, tomato, tuna, onion and mayonnaise

Serves 4; Preparation: 5 minutes; Cooking 12 minutes; Level of difficulty: Simple

Cook the conchiglie in a large pot of salted, boiling water until *al dente*. Drain very thoroughly. Transfer to a large salad bowl and toss well with half the oil. Set aside to cool. § Peel the eggs and cut into quarters lengthwise. Dice the tomatoes into bite-sized cubes. Break the tuna up by lightly pressing with a fork. Slice the white, bottom part of the shallot thinly. § When the pasta is cool, add the eggs, tomatoes, tuna, parsley, remaining oil, and mayonnaise. Sprinkle with salt, mix well, and serve.

Making Fresh Pasta at Home

Fresh pasta can be made either by hand or using a pasta machine. I strongly advise you not to use the pasta machines that mix the dough as well as cutting the pasta, since the finished product will be heavy and very inferior to handmade pasta. The first step in pasta making is to prepare the dough.

MIXING PLAIN PASTA DOUGH

For 4 generous servings you will need 400 g (12 oz) of plain white flour and 3 medium eggs. Place the flour in a mound on a flat work surface and hollow out a well in the centre. Break the eggs into the well one by one and beat lightly with a fork for 1-2 minutes. Pull some of the surrounding flour down over the egg mixture and gradually incorporate it. Continue until the mixture is no longer runny. Using your hands now, combine all the flour with the eggs. Work the mixture with your hands until it is smooth and moist, but quite firm.

To test the mixture for the correct consistency, press a clean finger into the dough. If it comes out easily and without any dough sticking to it, it is ready for kneading. If it is too moist, add more flour. If it is too dry, incorporate a little milk. Roll the mixture into a ball shape.

MIXING SPINACH PASTA DOUGH

For 4 generous servings you will need 250 g (8 oz) of plain white flour, 150 g (5 oz) of fresh spinach (or 100 g (3½ oz) thawed frozen spinach) and 2 large eggs. Cook the spinach in a little salted water until tender. Drain well and, when cool, squeeze out any excess moisture. Chop finely with a knife. Proceed as above for plain flour dough, working the spinach in together with the eggs.

KNEADING THE DOUGH

Clean the work surface of any excess dough or flour and lightly sprinkle with plain flour. Push down and forwards on the ball of pasta dough with the heel of your palm. Fold the slightly extended piece of dough in half, give it a quarter-turn, and repeat the process. Continue for about 10 minutes or until the dough is very smooth. Place the ball of pasta dough on a plate and cover with an upturned bowl. Leave to rest for at least 15-20 minutes.

ROLLING THE DOUGH OUT BY HAND

Place the ball of dough on a flat, clean work surface and flatten it a little with your hand. Place the rolling pin on the centre of the flattened ball and, applying light but firm pressure, roll the dough away from you. Give the ball a quarter-turn and repeat. When the dough has become a large round about 5 mm (¼ in) thick, curl the far edge over the pin while holding the edge closest to you with your hand. Gently stretch the pasta as you roll it all onto the pin. Unroll, give the dough a quarter-turn, and repeat. Continue rolling and stretching the dough until it is transparent.

ROLLING THE DOUGH OUT USING THE PASTA MACHINE

Divide the dough in to several pieces and flatten them slightly with your hand. Set the machine with its rollers at their widest, and run each piece through the machine. Reduce the rollers' width by one notch and repeat, reducing the rollers' width by one notch each time. Continue until all the pieces have gone through the machine at the thinnest roller setting.

Cutting the pasta by hand

For lasagna: cut the rolled out pasta into oblongs sheets about 8 x 30 cm (3 x 12 in).

For tagliolini, fettuccine, tagliatelle, and pappardelle: fold the hand-rolled pasta into a loose, flat roll. Using a large sharp knife, cut the roll into 2 mm (⅛ in) slices (for tagliolini), 5 mm (¼ in) slices (for fettuccine), 8 mm (⅓ in) slices (for tagliatelle), or 2 cm (¾ in) slices (for pappardelle). Unravel the pasta and lay it out flat on a clean tea towel. If you want fluted edges, use the wheel cutter on the pasta laid out flat. You will need a steady hand!

For maltagliati: fold the hand-rolled pasta into a loose, flat roll. Using a large sharp knife cut the pasta into rhomboid shapes. Separate the pieces and lay them out on a clean tea towel.

Cutting the pasta by machine

Cut the pieces of pasta lengthwise so that they are about 30 cm (12 in) long. Attach the cutters to the pasta machine and set the machine at the widths given above for the various types of pasta. Lay the cut pasta out on clean dry tea towels.

MAKING STUFFED PASTA

Pasta dough for stuffed pasta needs to be fairly moist, so try to work quickly and keep all the dough you are not using on a plate under an upturned dish.

For agnolotti, tortelli, and square-shaped ravioli: these are the easiest filled pasta shapes to make. Using a large sharp knife, cut the rolled out pasta into strips about 10 cm (4 in) wide. Place heaped teaspoonfuls of the mixture for the filling at intervals of about 5 cm (2 in) down the middle. Slightly moisten the edges of the pasta with your fingertips before folding them over and sealing them. Use a wheel cutter to cut between the stuffing. Run it along the sealed edges to give them a decorative, fluted edge as well.

For half-moon shaped ravioli: use a glass or biscuit cutter to cut the rolled out pasta into circular shapes. Place a teaspoonful of the filling at the centre, moisten the edges of the pasta with your fingertips and fold it over. Pinch the edges toegther with your fingers until they are well sealed. For fluted edges, run round each shape with the pastry cutter.

For tortellini: use a glass or biscuit cutter to cut the rolled out pasta into circular shapes. Place ½ teaspoonful of the filling mixture in the middle of each round. Moisten the edges of the pasta with your fingertips and fold the pasta over. Pick the tortellino up and twist it around your index finger until the edges meet. Pinch them together with your fingers and seal them.

For tortelloni: as above, but using a larger glass or a small bowl 8-9 cm (3½ in) in diameter and 1 teaspoonful of the filling mixture.

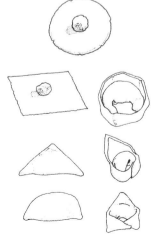

For cappelletti: using a large sharp knife, cut the rolled out pasta into strips about 5 cm (2 in) wide. Cut each strip into 5 cm (2 in) squares. Place ½ teaspoonfuls of the filling mixture in the centre of each. Fold the square diagonally in half to form a triangle. Moisten the edges slightly with your fingertips and seal them together. Pick up the triangle by one corner of its folded over side. Take the other folded over corner and wrap it around your index finger. Pinch the edges together to seal the pasta.

INDEX